Italian-American Family History

A Guide to
Researching and Writing About
Your Heritage

Sharon DeBartolo Carmack

Published by Genealogical Publishing Co., Inc.
1001 N. Calvert St., Baltimore, MD 21202
Library of Congress Catalogue Card Number 96-79437
International Standard Book Number 0-8063-1527-X
Made in the United States of America

Acknowledgments
and
Dedication

No author writes a book alone. Though the words (and errors) are mine, many people helped me get to this point. Katherine Scott Sturdevant, M.A., opened my eyes to social history and showed me how to blend it with family history. Just this aspect alone has provided me with a niche.

Reading drafts of this manuscript were a genealogist, an Italian genealogist, a librarian, a newspaper journalist, and an English teacher: Roger D. Joslyn, CG, FASG, Jonathan D. Galli, CGRS, Nancy Cominiello Reeves, M.A., Susan Rust, B.A., and Jeanne Gieck, M.A. Each one offered invaluable comments: "I don't get this." "Jeez, Chapter 3 was long." "I would be overwhelmed doing genealogy." "What does this mean?" "Oh, I get it."

And, no married author with children writes a book without jeopardizing her family life in one way or another. For their tolerance, patience, and never-ending support, I cannot thank my husband Steve and daughter Laurie enough. You both can come home now.

Finally, this book is dedicated to Abdul, who died 3 January 1997 at the age of nineteen years and nine months. I couldn't have written this without you on my lap.

SDC
January 1997

Contents

Ethan's top blew off with a bang. "You listen to me," he shouted. "Hawleys have been living here since the middle seventeen hundreds. You're a foreigner. You wouldn't know about that. We've been getting along with our neighbors and being decent all that time. If you think you can barge in from Sicily and change that, you're wrong. . . . My family's been here two hundred years. . . ."

"I don't talk very good English. You think Marullo is guinea name, wop name, dago name. My *genitori*, my name is maybe two, three thousand years old. Marullus is from Rome, Valerius Maximus tells about it. What's two hundred years?"

"You don't come from here."

"Two hundred years ago you don't neither."

John Steinbeck, *The Winter of Our Discontent*

Introduction

Per molte strade si va a Roma!

(There are many roads to Rome!)

J ust as there are many roads that lead to Rome, there are also many roads to researching family history, depending on your goals. The basics and starting point of family history research are the same whether your ancestors arrived in America in 1600 or 1900, or whether they came from Italy, Germany, Russia, England, or Ireland. You must begin with yourself and work backward in time: from the known to the unknown. So what makes the road to researching Italian ancestry different from German, or Russian, or English, or Irish? Italians and Italian Americans have customs, folkways, beliefs, and behaviors unique to their culture. Learning about these aspects will be the key to successfully researching and writing about your heritage.

Determining Your Research Goals

Successful Italian family history research depends greatly on your personal goals. Your goals will determine what research road you will take. Is your goal among the following:

- Trace your ancestry as far back as you can, gathering names and dates on pedigree charts?
- Find lost relatives?
- Trace your ancestry just to the immigrant generation?
- Write a book for your descendants, documenting as much information as you can find?
- Learn as much as possible about your ancestors and what their lives were like?
- Compile a family history that not only documents your heritage, but also tells a *story* about your ancestors?

Quite possibly, your goal is not even listed here; but it is important to stop and think about what you hope to accomplish in the course of researching your heritage.

My goal was a combination of these. I wanted to know everything I could about my ancestors and what their daily lives were like. What did they eat? What did they do everyday? How did they dress? Why did they leave Italy and come to America? Along with researching my ancestry as far back as I could, I wanted to publish a family history that not only documented my heritage, but also told a factual *story* about each generation and what their lives were like. So the research road I took led me to Italian-American *family history* and *placing my ancestors into historical perspective.*

Italian-American Family History and Historical Perspective

Family history research—thoroughly researching each generation and placing the family into historical perspective—is the current trend in genealogy, versus the more traditional gathering of names and dates and getting the lineage back as far as possible. When I decided to publish a book on one of my Italian lines, I wanted it to be more than just a book of names. I wanted it to be something the family would treasure and *read*. To me, the way to ensure this was to write a *narrative* family history—the factual story of my ancestors' lives. If this sounds like something you would like to do, too, you've come to the right place.

Family history research is similar to the recipe for baked lasagne:

Baked Lasagne

Step One: Ingredients

$^1/_2$ lb. ground meat	1 10-oz. pkg. lasagne noodles
$^1/_2$ lb. Italian sausage	1 lb. Ricotta cheese
1 clove garlic, minced	2 beaten eggs
1 Tbl. parsley	2 tea. salt
1 Tbl. basil	$^1/_2$ tea. pepper
$1^1/_2$ tea. salt	2 Tbl. parsley
2 cups chopped tomatoes	$^1/_2$ c. Parmesan cheese
2 6-oz. cans tomato paste	1 lb. Mozzarella cheese

Step Two: Combine Ingredients

Brown meat and sausage. Add next 6 ingredients to meat. Simmer uncovered until thick, 45 minutes to 1 hour, stirring occasionally. Cook noodles until tender; drain; rinse in cold water. Combine Ricotta cheese with next 5 ingredients. Place $1/2$ noodles in 13 x 9 x 2" baking dish; spread $1/2$ cheese mixture over noodles; add $1/2$ Mozzarella cheese and $1/2$ meat mixture. Repeat layers.

Step Three: Bake

Bake at 375° for 30 minutes. Let cool 5 minutes, then serve.

First you gather the ingredients. But each ingredient does not make baked lasagne. You must go on to the second step and mix and layer the ingredients. But this is still not baked lasagne. You have to go to that final step, baking, where all the ingredients and flavors blend and the cheeses melt. That's baked lasagne!

Now let's look at the recipe for family history:

Recipe for
Italian-American Family History

Step One: Ingredients

home sources
oral history
census schedules
passenger lists
naturalization records
wills/probate

land records
church records
vital records
school records
social histories

Step Two: Combine Ingredients

Review and analyze slowly all records pertaining to your ancestors. Add the relevant Italian-American social history. Mix family and social history until well blended.

Step Three: Bake

Write a narrative family history that is both a legacy and an interesting read. Serve.

The ingredients are the sources you consult in your research project. But the sources by themselves do not make a family history. In the second step, you analyze each record, comparing and combining information from all of the sources. But this is still not your family history. You must go that final step, writing the narrative, where all of the sources meld into an interesting story. That's family history!

What Can You Accomplish Within America's Shores?

When I began researching my Italian ancestry in 1985, there wasn't much information available to help Italian Americans trace their roots. The one book I did find made it seem impossible unless I was able to hire someone in Italy or go there myself—neither of which I could afford. Eleven years later, I find myself pretty much in the same predicament. I still can't afford to go to Italy, and I still can't afford to hire someone there. But I have, at least to my satisfaction, researched several of my Italian lines as far back as the late eighteenth century without leaving America.

Unlike eleven years ago when I started, today you can do a majority of your research from America—enough to publish your Italian family history. You may be in a situation like me—financially unable to visit your ancestral homeland to do the research yourself or to hire someone there—but you'd like to get something compiled for future generations before you die. Well, you *can* do it, right now, and right here from the good old U.S. of A.

I don't want to raise any false hopes, though. We must be realistic. From America you may only be able to get your ancestry back in Italy to about the early 1800s or late 1700s. Or you may not even be able to get beyond the immigrant ancestor who came to America in 1905. (Of course, this is also true for descendants with other ethnic backgrounds.) But if you feel you would like to get something written and published soon, then this book can show you how to leave a treasured legacy for your descendants. And, if you do get to Italy in the future and can extend your lineage further, you can always write a supplement.

Drowning in the Ocean

Because all of your genealogical research projects will begin from the same starting point—you—the research for the first one, two, three, or maybe four generations back to the immigrants will be solely in American records. Too many people who descend from early twentieth-century immigrants tend to skip these important generations, thinking they already know all about their parents, grandparents, and perhaps great-grandparents. They are anxious to cross the ocean and find their ancestors in the Old Country. Please don't "generation hop." Too many people have drowned in the ocean when they did. When you skip generations in America, you increase your chances of tracing the wrong ancestry in Italy, especially if you don't have enough information from American sources. For example, what may be a unique Italian name in America could be the John Smith of Italy. If you don't have sufficient identifying data on a person, you may not recognize your ancestor in the Italian records and end up connecting to the wrong person.

The best clues to solving your research problems and learning as much as possible about the immigrant are in the community or communities where he or she resided in America. Remember, too, that our parents' and grandparents' lives in America need thorough documentation. Their life experiences were just as dramatic and exciting as those who were left behind in Italy. In some ways, the Italian-American generations are more fascinating, especially when you consider all the changes these families went through in adapting to life in a new land.

While the main emphasis of this book is the immigrant and American generations—the *Italian-American* aspect—it also bridges the ocean and shows you how to do as much research as possible in Italian records from America. Between the late 1870s and 1930s more than five million Italians immigrated to America; 80 percent originated from southern Italy. Therefore, this book's focus is mainly for those with southern Italian heritage—those with ancestry in the *Mezzogiorno*: the regions of Abruzzi, Molise, Apulia, Basilicata, Calabria, Campania, parts of Latium, and the island of Sicily.

What This Book Will and Won't Do for You

In sum, the scope of this book is to show you how to

- Start your Italian-American family history research
- Evaluate American records for information specific to Italian-American researchers
- Research Italian-American historical perspective
- Use historical perspective for better research success and to ultimately write a narrative
- Find and use Italian records in America
- Learn more about Italy from America—history, culture, customs, folklore, and lifestyles
- Blend your family history research with historical perspective to write a narrative about your ancestors
- Publish, market, and distribute your Italian-American family history book

Because there are already numerous, good, general how-to books on genealogy and family history research (see end of the bibliography), I will not be discussing in detail how to find and use traditional genealogical records such as censuses, vital records, passenger arrival lists, land deeds, church records, and probate. Instead, I am going to point out information contained in many of these sources that is important to you as an Italian-American researcher.

Currently, there are two excellent books available on how to locate and use Italian records, and I highly recommend both: John Philip Colletta's *Finding Italian Roots* (Baltimore: Genealogical Publishing Co., 1993) and Trafford R. Cole's *Italian Genealogical Records: How to Use Italian Civil, Ecclesiastical, and Other Records in Family History Research* (Salt Lake City: Ancestry Publishing, 1995).

So if your goal is to research your Italian ancestry from America and to write a narrative family history about your heritage, you're on the right road, whether it ultimately leads you to Rome or somewhere else in Italy.

Chapter 1
Leaving Italy and Coming to America

Arrivederci Italia!

(Good-bye Italy!)

The Italian Presence in America Before the Civil War

Because the Italian presence in America was so obvious
after the 1880s, little is written about Italians who came
to America during earlier centuries. What has generally
been published concerns noteworthy individuals of Italian de-
scent: Columbus, Giovanni Caboto, Amerigo Vespucci, Francesco
Vigo, and Filippo Mazzei. There were also a significant number,
perhaps some of your ancestors, who immigrated during the
colonial and national periods. Those who arrived before the
mid-1800s were primarily northern Italians—skilled artisans,
tradesmen, musicians, scientists, and political refugees. Around
1656–57, a group of about 167 Protestant Italians, known as Wal-
densians, came to the American colonies. These immigrants came
from the valleys of Piedmont between Turin and Modane, near
the border of France, and settled in New York, Delaware, Virginia,
the Carolinas, and Georgia.

More arrivals from the Piedmont area of Italy came to the
colony of Savannah, Georgia, in the 1730s in an attempt to estab-
lish a silk manufacturing center. While the silk colony ultimately
failed by 1790, other Italian silk industries flourished in Connecti-
cut, Pennsylvania, and New York.

Some of the Italians who settled in colonial Virginia migrated
and settled first in England for a generation or two before coming to America. One such family was the Taliaferros. Genealogical and historical publications disagree as to whether the family
originated from Florence, Venice, or Genoa, but it is documented
that they migrated to England first, then came to Virginia in the
1640s. One historian stated that "any white Virginian having Vir-

15

ginian ancestry of at least three generations will be in some way related to the Taliaferros." Because the Italian name "Taliaferro" was difficult for Virginia tongues, the name has come to be pronounced "Toliver."

Italian immigrants further south in America can be traced in New Orleans as early as 1718. Some of these earlier arrivals, whose names may have been inadvertently changed to French spellings, were military deserters or tobacco smugglers. Others came as silkworkers, laborers, shoemakers, and farmers.

Since there are no official compiled statistics of the numbers of Italian settlers prior to the 1880s, historians have mostly had to identify Italian origins based on surnames found in records. Italian-American historians agree that this is not a foolproof method, however, since names that may appear Italian can conceal other origins. For example, the Jerdone family was from Scotland, and the name Bolito (Bolithoe) is actually English. Often, if the immigrant was English of Italian extraction, the records do not designate Italian ancestry. When a nationality is mentioned, though, it may not be "Italian," but may be more specific to the region of origin (Genoa, Florence, Turin). Since Italy was not unified until after the 1860s, the people considered themselves citizens of a town or region rather than a nation. Francesco Vigo, who served as a fur trader during the American Revolutionary War, is found in some records as Genoese and in some as Italian. On the other hand, Robert Taliaferro, the immigrant to Virginia from England, is listed in American records as English.

Although Italians did not arrive in mass numbers before the Civil War, their presence left an impact on American culture. Even their food became a part of colonial society. By the 1700s there was already a market for Italian food products. Such items as olive oil, wines, pasta, Parmesan cheese, sausages, and anchovies were imported and in demand in the American colonies.

Italian Immigration After the Civil War

A significant influx of Italians to America began in the latter part of the nineteenth century. Beginning in about the 1870s, the majority of arrivals in America came from southern Italy and consisted of unskilled laborers who helped build railroads, canals, and streets. They originated from the *Mezzogiorno:* the regions of Abruzzi, Molise, Campania, Basilicata, Apulia, Calabria, parts of Latium, and the island of Sicily. The peak years of their arrival were between 1880 and 1920.

Leaving Italy was no doubt a difficult decision for many since their roots had been buried in the Italian soil for centuries. The emigrants were what historians term "push migrants," those who may not have really wanted to leave but were being forced out by unfavorable conditions in the homeland. Some reasons to leave were low wages, a moribund argarian economy, poor health conditions, industrial backwardness and stagnation, a lingering feudal system, heavy taxation, a high cost of living, and corruption in local and church governments. Added to this, southern Italy experienced many natural disasters, including droughts, volcanic eruptions, and earthquakes. Malnutrition and epidemics of cholera and malaria increased the mortality rate.

Birds of Passage and Chain Migration

Finding work became more and more difficult in southern Italy. Many of those who left for America had planned to stay only long enough to earn money and return to Italy to buy land rather than pay rent to absentee landlords. These "birds of passage," or seasonal migrants, made the transatlantic voyage several times, working a few months in America and returning to Italy in time for the harvest. Italians were among the top three ethnic groups with the highest return migration rate: 30 percent went back to Italy within five years of arrival in America. In 1903, for example, more than 214,000 Italians came to this county, but about 78,000 went back to Italy the same year.

Because return migration was so popular among Italians, it is really important for you to check passenger arrival indexes and lists beyond the first time you find your ancestor. Albino DeBartolo is a typical example. He went back to Italy twice over a period of six years before deciding to settle in America and bring over his family in 1913. In fact, you should check all the major ports of arrival for possible returnees in your ancestry (New York, Boston, Philadelphia, New Orleans, Baltimore). Felice Vallarelli came to America in 1906 through the Port of New York. He went back to Italy and returned to America in 1916, this time arriving at Boston. Significant gaps of more than two years in the births of a family's children are a good indication that Papa may have been away from home and might be a bird of passage.

For most Italians, however, the higher wages in America were an enticement to stay here and resettle, so they sent for their families after earning enough money to do so, usually in three to five years. Along with better wages, what drew more and more southern Italians to leave their homeland was the availability of jobs and the opportunity to own land here. In what historians have termed "chain migration," villagers who already immigrated encouraged others to join them by sending them money and providing temporary lodging for the newcomers. Some of these chains were so strong that nearly an entire village might follow over a period of years. The town of Roseto, Pennsylvania, for example, was settled almost entirely by people who had left Roseto Valforte, Apulia.

Others, unsure of how to find work and accommodations in America, might be aided by a *padrone*. The *padrone* (labor contractor) scouted for potential emigrants in their native villages in Italy, paying passage and guaranteeing a job in exchange for paying off the debt with interest over a period of years. This method was similar to the colonial indenture system but was actually more like the redemption system popularized by German arrivals in Pennsylvania. The Italian immigrant repaid (with interest) his redeemer with a portion of his salary instead of becoming a virtual slave for four to seven years. Contract labor was outlawed by the United States government in 1885; however, *padroni* continued to operate underground.

Ports of Arrival

One incentive for the mass immigration of southern Italian peasants to America beginning in the 1870s was steamships. Passage across the Atlantic took only about ten days to two weeks, as opposed to five weeks to three months by sail. This made migration and return migration more feasible and economical. Most southern Italians came by "steerage," or third class. Steerage was so named because it was a large compartment located below deck near the steering mechanism. A one-way steerage ticket cost between $10 and $35, depending on the year; second class was about $40, and first was $80.

About one-quarter of all Italian emigrants who traveled to the United States in steerage left from the Port of Naples. Other ports of departure were Genoa and Palermo in Sicily. Of all the ships that left Europe, seven out of every ten headed for the Port of New York, making it the busiest port between 1880 and 1920. Other popular ports were Boston, Baltimore, Philadelphia, New Orleans, and Galveston. Each had its own immigrant processing center, like New York's famous Ellis Island (a discussion of passenger arrival lists and Ellis Island records can be found in Chapter 3: Searching U.S. Sources for Clues Specific to Italian-American Research, and in Appendix A: An Example of an Italian-American Family History Narrative).

Settlement Patterns

Migrations to a new locality followed certain patterns. People from a particular region, city, or village in Italy settled in specific regions, cities, or even specific city blocks in America. With constant invading foreign powers throughout Italy's history, the peasants realized that the only people upon whom they could trust and depend were their family, first, and their fellow villagers, second. Each village celebrated its own festivals and spoke its own dialect. There was very little mingling between one village and the next. Italian provinces often had little in common with each other, and even though Italy was unified by the 1860s, the people still considered themselves citizens of a town, not a nation. They weren't leaving Italy; they were leaving their village. They were Baresi, Genovesi, Avellinesi, Neapolitans, Syracusans, Calabrians. They did not become "Italians" until they arrived in America. So when they settled here, they grouped together in ethnic enclaves by village or region of origin with people who could speak their dialect and were familiar with their customs.

One example is St. Louis, Missouri's "Dago Hill." The people in this area came primarily from Lombardy and Sicily. In New York City, specific city blocks housed people from like villages. Mulberry Bend was occupied by Neapolitans; Baxter Street near Five Points drew Genoese; Houston and Spring streets housed Sicilians; and 112th Street of East Harlem attracted villagers from Avigliano. In Pittsburgh, the Panther Hollow district was dominated by people from Abruzzi. Sicilians from four villages—Santo Stefano Quisquina, Alessandria della Rocca, Cianciana, and Contessa Entellina—made up a community in Tampa, Florida. Another Sicilian village near Catania found a new home in Galveston, Texas.

These specific settlement patterns illustrate the importance of learning about your ancestor's neighborhood, especially if you are uncertain about your ancestor's place of origin. Researching the neighbors and discovering what village they left in Italy would be the logical starting place for your research.

Like other ethnic groups, many Italians became mobile as they assimilated into American society. Landlords raising rents forced many immigrants to move within the ethnic enclave. Those who prospered financially bought their own homes. One historian has estimated that families moved approximately every ten years, either from one tenement to another within the same city or from the city to the suburbs. The Banoni family lived in Manhattan at 239 Mulberry Street in 1900; by 1910 they had moved to 156 Sullivan Street. The Ebetino family of Rye, New York, began life in America at 128 Maple Avenue; five years later the family is found at 16 Nursery Lane, where they remained for ten to fifteen years; then they bought a home located on West Purdy Avenue; finally, about twenty years later, they moved to 90 Theodore Fremd Avenue.

Name Changes and Prejudice

Part of understanding our ancestors and the difference between research success and failure is learning what motivated them to behave in certain ways. Why did they leave Italy? Where did they go? And equally important, *how were they treated when they got to a new locality?* Prejudice could influence an Italian immigrant in many ways that could affect your genealogical research. For example, your ancestor may have been "forced" to "Americanize" his name because he needed to hide his origins in order to get a job.

Italians were constant targets of prejudice—victims of *nativism* or antiforeignism. The term nativism was coined about 1840 when this country experienced a dramatic increase in Irish and German immigration. The antiforeignist feeling was rekindled in the 1880s when Italians and other southern Europeans began arriving in mass numbers. These new immigrants had a high birthrate, and nativists feared the loss of Anglo-Saxon dominance. More than half of the incoming Italians were illiterate, and almost all were Catholic. They were also at the bottom of the labor chain. And, nativists believed, Italians were bloodthirsty criminals, so they became the target of prejudice and violence. In New Orleans, for example, eleven Italians were lynched on 14 March 1891 for alleged murders, followed by three Italians lynched on 9 August 1896 who were accused of murdering whites in Hahnville, and five more were lynched in Tallulah in 1899. One Italian woman said, "I thought life in America would be different. I was poor in Italy, and I'm poor here. I learned to be afraid here. I never was afraid before." (There were advantages to nativism and prejudice—at least for us as genealogical researchers. Because of the mass arrivals of Italians and other groups, the government started keeping more detailed records. Hence you will find that records such as censuses, passengers lists, and naturalizations, to name a few, offer more information as more foreigners immigrated here.)

To avoid negative reactions, many Italians tried to hide their origins. Some Italian women who applied for clerical jobs called themselves French, Spanish, or Turkish. The most common way to obscure their origins, of course, was to change their names. There were many reasons to do so, but in some cases name changes were done for them. Though many descendants report that their immigrant ancestor's name was changed by officials on Ellis Island, I have yet to find a documented case of this. More than likely, the immigrant himself changed it to escape prejudice and to "fit in," or perhaps schools changed the children's names because the foreign ones were too hard to pronounce.

Naturally, name changes cause problems for genealogists who do not have family stories or other sources to lead them to the original name. The change may be a literal translation: Francesco Bianco to Frank White or Giuseppe Verdi to Joe Green. It may also be a shortened version of the name: Salvatore DeBartolo to Sal Bart. At the least, some persons may have kept the same initials as their original name. Here are a few examples of "Americanized" versions or translations of first names:

Albino	Albert
Carlo	Charles, Chuck
Felice	Philip, Phil
Francesco	Frank
Fortunato	Frederick, Fred
Giacchiano	Jack
Giovanni	John
Giuseppe	Joseph, Joe
Michele	Michael, Mike
Paolo	Paul
Pasquale	Patsy, Pat
Raffaele	Ralph
Salvatore	Sal, Tore
Vincenzo	Vinnie, Vincent

To succeed in tracing your Italian ancestry you must know at least two things: your original Italian name and your family's place of origin in Italy. Though you may already know these details from family stories, the next chapter is still an important step that should not be skipped. If you don't know the original family name and the village in Italy, the following chapter may unlock the mystery.

Chapter 2
Starting Your Search

Un segreto della famiglia

(Family secrets)

Italians love to keep secrets. The content of the secret is not important. Italians believe that secrets preserve the boundaries of the family, establishing who is accepted and who is not. But it seems to go beyond that. My grandmother took many secrets to her grave—like why she broke off all communication with her husband's family after his death. It wasn't until many years after her funeral that I discovered I had living relatives on that side of the family.

If your Italian relatives are like mine, you may find that they may be unwilling to talk about certain aspects of their lives. They may also find your interest in the past puzzling. "Why do you want to know about people who are long dead? We left Italy because life was miserable. It's best to forget it." Prodding them to tell secrets may only serve to heighten their mistrust. If you gain their trust, they may be more likely to open up to you.

Oral History

The importance of conducting oral history interviews cannot be stressed enough in Italian-American family history. Many of you are fortunate because the immigrant generation is still living. (A claim a *Mayflower* descendant certainly can't make!) Even though your grandparents or great-grandparents (whoever the immigrants were) may be gone, their siblings, cousins, or other relatives would be good sources of information about life in Italy, places of origin, original names, and why and when your immigrant ancestors came to America.

When I was a baby genealogist, I was a good little girl and interviewed my Italian grandmother, asking her questions like the names of her parents, when she was born, when they were born, when they came to America, where they came from in Italy, etc. Then, as advised in the genealogical how-to books, I verified everything she told me in original documents.

I hated doing oral history interviewing. My grandmother hated being interviewed.

My next interviewing experience was many years later with her cousins, after my grandmother had passed away—three spinster ladies. I followed the same procedure in asking for names, dates, and places. I was such a pest about it, they finally told me, "Please don't ask us any more questions. We've told you everything we know."

It didn't take me long to realize that oral history interviewing wasn't a pleasant experience for anyone. So I stopped interviewing relatives after that. What was the point? From my experiences, I believed that interviewing relatives was essentially a waste of time: Why bother asking questions if you're going to find the information in a record somewhere anyway?

Today, I do have regrets. It wasn't until I learned how *social historians* conduct oral history interviews that I realized I was going about it all wrong.

I discovered that the purpose of an interview was not necessarily to ask questions about information I probably *would* find in a record, but to ask questions about things I *wouldn't* find in a record. Of course, if you don't know the original Italian name and where in Italy the family originated, these are top priority questions, as well as the time and place of immigration. But also keep in mind questions like the following:

- Did you or your family experience any prejudice for being Italian?
- What was your relationship like with your father?
- What did the house you grew up in look like?
- How did your family celebrate holidays?
- What kinds of foods did you eat?
- How did your mother prepare meals?

The answers to these questions, unfortunately, are in the grave with my grandmother. I will never know the answers because I can't find them in a record, as I can names, dates, and places.

The happy side to the story, however, is that when I next approached my grandmother's cousins for an interview I was better prepared, and *we all enjoyed ourselves*. I asked things such as

- How big was the house you grew up in?
- Can you draw me a floor plan?
- What did the furniture look like?
- What did you eat for breakfast, lunch, dinner?
- How was it cooked?
- Did you eat dessert every night?
- What did you eat on special occasions?
- Where did your mother have her babies?
- Did she nurse them?

But suppose many of your older relatives are gone? Or everyone in the immigrant generation has passed on? How can you still obtain some of the same information? The immigrant's children might be able to relate some stories their parents told them about life in the Old Country or their experience of coming to America. If the focus is to learn what life was like during the immigrant's day, and she's gone, perhaps there are others who can give details. Search out friends, neighbors, and contemporaries of your immigrant ancestor who might still be alive. Along with being able to tell you about your ancestor, they might have had similar lifestyles and experiences. Another helpful person might be the historian of the town where your ancestors settled.

Okay, so what about accuracy and verifying information? We know that stories handed down from generation to generation tend to get distorted. It is true that human memory has shortcomings. It is prone to selection, lapses, mistakes, and fabrications. But aren't all sources subject to error? Have you ever found several consecutive census enumerations on one family to be 100 percent factual? Have you ever found a birth record to be in error? Have you ever found an obituary with errors? Or a tombstone? Oral history is no less reliable than any of these sources. In some cases, it may be more reliable and accurate than a recorded document. Who better to tell you about what it was like to process through Ellis Island than someone who actually did it?

Most genealogy how-to books put oral history interviewing at the beginning stage of tracing your family history. Mine's no different; however, I believe oral history interviewing should happen at least twice: first, when you start your family history research, and second, after you have already done quite a bit of research. By conducting an interview after you've done some research you can speak more intelligently about the family, and you can bring photocopies of documents with you to the interview that may trigger more memories.

When I re-interviewed my grandmother's cousin Isabel, I brought along a copy of the ship's passenger list that listed her as a child when she came to America. She was quite tickled, and even more willing to talk to me when I told her she could keep the copy. While this document was common to me and something I looked at frequently, it hadn't occurred to me that she would never have seen it.

The drawback of having all this genealogical knowledge when you do the interview is that you have a really strong urge to correct your relatives. But remember, your goal is to gain information, not correct, debate, or educate them. My great uncle still believes he came to America on the ship *Ancona*. I have documented proof—the passenger list—that says he came on the ship *Verona*. He refuses to believe me. Perhaps he was supposed to travel on the *Ancona* and somehow ended up on the *Verona*. So what? What's wrong with letting him believe he's correct? In my files, I've put what I have documented proof of.

Another advantage of doing some preliminary research is that you'll be able to ask questions about any discrepancies you may find in records. In my great-grandfather's will, he leaves a savings bond to each of his three grandchildren: my Uncle Albert, my Aunt Lucy, and my father, Salvatore. In the will, he calls the first two by their Italian names: Albino and Lucia; the third by an American name: "Jack." My great-grandfather stated that these are all of the children of his son, Giuseppe, so I know he was referring to my uncle, my aunt, and my father. But my father's name is Salvatore—always has been. The only nickname I ever heard him called was "Tore," the shortened version of Salvatore. Fortunately, my father is still alive and was able to explain the mystery. His grandfather called him "Jack" because my father resembled his maternal grandfather, Giacchino, or Jack, and was dubbed the nickname as a child. This was the only person who ever called him that.

There are many techniques and items to consider when doing an oral history interview, such as how long the interview should last, how to behave during an interview, getting permission to use the material from the interview, whether to tape the interview or not, how to transcribe the tape, and what to do with the information. For more details, you should consult one of the many guidebooks listed in the bibliography on oral history interviewing.

Keep in mind that when you finally write your family history, your oral history interviews should be supplemented with your genealogical research and with social history (see Chapter 4: Researching Italian-American Historical Perspective; and Chapter 9: Blending Social and Family History Research to Write a Narrative).

Home Sources

My family never kept anything. As a matter of fact, when my grandmother moved from New York to California in her golden years, she even tossed out all of the old family photographs. I hope you have more luck in finding home sources than I've had. While you're visiting your relatives for an oral history interview, this is a good time to rummage through their house for genealogical miscellany and other clues that will help your research. Of course, you don't want to start searching through their belongings without their permission! It would probably be better to ask them if they have items such as

- Passports
- Citizenship papers
- Funeral prayer cards
- A family Bible
- Birth, marriage, or death certificates
- Old photographs
- Letters or postcards of correspondence with relatives in Italy
- Diaries or journals
- Deeds
- Family recipes
- Objects brought from Italy

If they have originals of some of these documents or photographs, ask them if they wouldn't mind your taking them to the corner print shop and making photocopies for your files. If you're into computer technology, a laptop computer with a hand-held scanner is another way of copying documents and photographs. Above all, however, you do not want to cause damage to originals in any way. Repeated exposure to photocopiers and scanners could cause long-term, harmful effects on old paper and photographs. You may want to bring along a focusable 35mm camera to the interview. You can take pictures of records and photographs, as well as copying the information by hand or into your laptop. These camera copies may not be as good as a professional's, but they're better than nothing.

You may even have inherited some of these items and have them in your own home. Look them over carefully. Once again, if you do not know the original Italian name or place of origin, these items—or others you may find—may give you that information or provide you with clues. Certainly take note of people who may have witnessed any documents or who were correspondents. These people may still be alive and willing to talk to you; or perhaps in researching the witnesses you will find the village of origin, since the witnesses likely came from the same place or region as your ancestors.

Like oral history interviewing, you may find it beneficial to comb through your house and your relatives' again after you have done some research. The information you find in the records may lead you back to home sources with a new eye for clues.

Chapter 3
Searching U.S. Sources for Clues Specific to Italian-American Research

Di dov'è lei?

(Where are you from?)

As discussed in the introduction, the purpose of this chapter is not to tell you how to use genealogical records per se. Its purpose is to focus on U.S. sources that you will commonly consult in tracing your Italian ancestry and to point out items of particular interest that will help in your search and propel you back to Italy. Remember, the information you need to identify your immigrant ancestors in Italian records will come from American sources. Think of every possible document your ancestor could have created or been listed in during his or her lifetime, then seek it. Although a single record may not answer specifically where your ancestor originated or his or her date of arrival in America, you just never know what it will tell you or what clues it will yield. Leave no stone unturned.

Not all types of records are discussed here, just the most commonly searched documents.

For more detailed information on record groups, research, and methodology, consult one of the guidebooks listed in the bibliography.

Compiled Family Histories

Although you are unlikely to find one on your Italian family, it never hurts to check and see if someone has already compiled a family history. In the past, the trend was for genealogists to write books about their colonial forebears or ancestors who came to America prior to the Civil War. Though it is now becoming popular to publish genealogies on recent immigrants, these books are still few in number. *You* will be the one doing future generations a favor when you write and publish your family history.

Surname Dictionaries

Surname dictionaries like Joseph G. Fucilla's *Our Italian Surnames* may give you some clues to province of origin, telling where your Italian last name was most prevalent in Italy. Surname dictionaries published in Italy and found in the Family History Library in Salt Lake City may give even more specific information.

Federal Population (Census) Schedules

Census records are one of the first records you will check in searching for your Italian ancestors. Population schedules are widely available, offer lots of valuable information, and most of them have indexes, making them easy to use.

An enumeration of America's population has been taken every ten years since 1790; however, because of the Privacy Laws, only those schedules that are seventy-two years old or older may be accessed by the public, the 1920 census being the most recently opened. (Other federal record groups have different privacy restrictions. See *Guide to Genealogical Research in the National Archives* for details.) Early censuses (1790–1840) list only the names of the heads of the household. From 1850 to the present, however, every individual in the household is listed by name. Information varied from decade to decade, with the schedules during the peak immigration years containing the most information (the advantage of having recent immigrants!). The schedules for 1890 were virtually destroyed in a fire.

Guides to the enumeration schedules and indexes are available through National Archives publications. Census records may be viewed on microfilm at the National Archives and its regional branches, and at the Family History Library in Salt Lake City and by microfilm rental through its family history centers. You may also rent microfilm of censuses and other federal records and view it in your home if you own a microfilm reader, or you may take films to your local library. Two companies offer this service: American Genealogical Lending Library, P.O. Box 329, Bountiful, UT 84011-0329; and the National Archives Microfilm Rental Program, P.O. Box 30, Annapolis Junction, MD 20701-0030. Many local libraries have censuses for their state; for instance, Penrose

Library in Colorado Springs has all Colorado censuses. Also, censuses through 1880 are available on CD-ROM from Broderbund Software, Banner Blue Division, 39500 Stevenson Place, Fremont, CA 94539-3103.

The 1870 census was the first to ask people if their parents were foreign born, but it did not name the country; only a check mark was placed in that column. The 1880 enumeration asked for the birthplace of each individual in the household and for the parents of each individual. The majority of enumerators, as instructed by the Census Bureau, recorded only the name of the country, but some may have noted specific towns or regions. Beginning in 1900, columns were added that related more specifically to immigration. The schedules for 1900 and 1910 provided columns for "if foreign born, year of immigration and whether naturalized." In 1920, columns were added for "if foreign born, year of immigration to the U.S., whether naturalized, and year of naturalization." Abbreviations used in the naturalization column include "Na" for naturalized, "Pa" for first papers filed, "Al" for alien, or "NR" for not reported.

If you have problems finding your ancestor in a census index, you may want to check the actual census, going page by page, for the county or town where the family lived. If they lived in a major city like New York, Boston, or Chicago, you will need to obtain an exact address from city directories (discussed later) in order to determine the enumeration district. Otherwise, you could spend years going page-by-page. If it is a small community, however, it is well worth the effort. I found my great-grandfather, Salvatore Ebetino, enumerated on the 1910 census as Salvatori Abitai through a page-by-page search. Keep in mind that the census taker spelled names phonetically, and immigrants had heavy accents. The nativist enumerator was certainly too busy to ask for the spelling of a name, and he assumed that immigrants were too ignorant and couldn't spell them if asked.

Ideally, you want to find your ancestors in all censuses in which they could have been enumerated. You never know what you may find since the information will vary from census year to census year and may be inconsistent.

Also, be sure to take note of the neighbors—not just who lived next door, but in the same tenement building, or even in the same apartment. Some of these people may be relatives of your ancestors (cousins, uncles, aunts) or, at the least, they may have been people your ancestors knew in their Italian village. Remember, if you are having trouble determining the village of origin or time of arrival for your own ancestors, research the neighbors. Perhaps they named their village of origin or time of arrival in a record, which will give you a possible starting place and time period to hunt for your ancestors. On the neighbors' passenger list, in particular, they could have named your ancestor as someone they were going to join in America.

State Censuses

Just as the federal government took a count of the population every ten years, some states also took an enumeration in between "census years." New York, for example, took state censuses beginning in 1825. Unlike the federal government, which closes its censuses to the public for seventy-two years, states determine their own privacy restrictions. If your immigrant ancestors lived in New York in the early twentieth century, the 1905, 1915, and 1925 state censuses will be helpful in your research since they give immigration and naturalization information. In the 1925 schedule there are columns for number of years in the United States, whether a citizen or alien, and if naturalized, when and where. These as well as many other state censuses are available through the Family History Library, as well as at state archives and repositories. Consult Ann S. Lainhart's *State Census Records* for a state-by-state listing of what state censuses are available.

Passenger Arrival Lists

Before you can begin to search passenger arrival lists, you must know your ancestor's original Italian name, an approximate age at immigration, the port of arrival, and at least the year of immigration. The more specific the date, of course, the better.

Original passenger arrival lists, 1820–1957, have been microfilmed and are available through the National Archives, the Family History Library in Salt Lake City and its branches, and through loan from American Genealogical Lending Library and the National Archives (see information under Census Records). A guide published by the National Archives, *Immigrant and Passenger Arrivals: A Select Catalog of National Archives Microfilm Publications* details the availability of records and indexes for each port.

Official immigration records begin in 1820, although records for some individual ports may predate this. Created at the port of departure or enroute to America, the early records, known as Customs Passenger Lists, from 1820 to about 1891, were kept primarily for statistical purposes, so they contain relatively limited information for family historians: name of ship and its master, port of embarkation, date and port of arrival, each passenger's name, sex, age, occupation, and nationality.

The records created after 1891 are referred to as Immigration Passenger Lists and span 1891 to the present. The United States Privacy Laws for passenger information restricts access to those records created after 1957. Information varied over the decades, and as the influx of immigrants became greater, more details were recorded on the arrival lists: last residence; final destination in the United States; if going to join a relative, the relative's name and address; personal description; place of birth; and name and address of closest living relative in native country.

There are several published sources that will assist you with the use of passenger arrival lists. For a general overview of the subject, see John Philip Colletta's *They Came in Ships,* and for a more comprehensive discussion, see Michael Tepper's *American Passenger Arrival Records: A Guide to the Records of Immigrants Arriving at American Ports by Sail and Steam.* If the name of a ship is known, but only an approximate date of arrival at the U.S. port, consult the *Morton Allan Directory of European Passenger Steamship Arrivals.* This book is arranged by year, giving names of ships and their ports and dates of arrival. For example, on an immigrant's declaration of intention, he may state that he came through the Port of New York and arrived on the ship *Italia* in 1905, but no specific date is given. Looking in the *Morton Allan Directory,* you can determine the exact dates that ship docked in New York in 1905 and narrow your search. Or sometimes the immigrant will give an exact date, but it is off by several days or months. It may save you time in the long run to check the *Morton Allan Directory* first when you have a date of arrival, just to confirm that a ship docked on a particular date at a particular port.

Ira Glazier and P. William Filby's ten-volume series *Italians to America: Lists of Passengers Arriving at U.S. Ports, 1880–1899* covers the major American ports of arrival, but primarily the port of New York. Data were taken from the original passenger lists compiled at the port of embarkation and filed once the ship docked in America. Most of the lists deal with ships that left ports in Italy—Naples, Genoa, and Palermo—but Glazier and Filby also have included those Italians sailing on ships that departed from other European ports. Along with a surname index to every volume, the information contained gives the name of the vessel, ports of departure and arrival, date of arrival, name of passenger, age, sex, occupation, village or province of origin, and destination (when available). As already stated, most of the arrival lists for the 1880s contain scanty information; places of origin may simply be recorded as Italy. Under the column "village or province of origin" a listing of "unknown" is typical.

This series of books offers convenient access to a previously unindexed group of records; however, be aware that transcription errors occurred during the compilation. For example, in a random comparison of a ship's list transcribed in *Italians to America* with the original list on microfilm available through the National Archives, I noted several transcription errors. For the ship *Utopia*, which left Naples and arrived at New York on 23 April 1883, I found that the twenty-five-year-old E. Cassiere, a female passenger, is recorded as a servant in *Italians to America*; on the original list (National Archives microfilm M237, roll 464), she is a maid. Ant. Gersosimo is listed in the book as one-year-old; on the microfilmed list he is fifteen months old. G. Mennella, a male aged forty-four, is of "unknown" occupation in Glazier and Filby's work; on the microcopy, his occupation is "interpreter." Sav. Rubetro appears as a forty-eight-year-old laborer on both the transcription and the original; but the transcription omits his death aboard the *Utopia* on 21 April 1883 of pneumonia. This is an important detail if Sav. Rubetro is *your* ancestor. These examples reinforce the standard rule: you should always go beyond the conveniently published record to verify its accuracy against the original.

When married Italian women came to this country, they were often recorded on passenger lists by their *maiden names*. This was the custom in Italy for all legal documents; women were known by their family/birth name. (Keep this in mind particularly when you are searching Italian death records.) Therefore, on American passenger arrival indexes, look for your female ancestors under their maiden names. If you do not know the maiden name, but children also came with the woman, the children will be recorded and indexed with the husband's surname. Obviously, this is an excellent way to discover maiden names.

Passenger lists were filed at the port where the ship first landed in the United States. Your ancestor may have landed at the Port of Boston, then took a train to a final destination in New York. Or the ship may have stopped at other ports after docking first in Boston. Be sure to check other ports if your ancestor is not found where you think he or she should be.

The columns on the passenger lists after 1893, under the heading "If ever in the United States before, when, where, and for how long," will indicate whether you are dealing with a "bird of passage"; and "If going to join a relative, the relative's name, address, and relationship," may alert you to relatives with whom you may not be familiar, who preceded your ancestor to America.

After 1906, the lists included a physical description of all passengers, giving their height, complexion, color of hair and eyes, and identifying marks. It was on such a list that I discovered that my sixty-two-year-old great-great grandmother was only four feet tall! Another extremely important column on the post-1906 lists is "place of birth," which gives names of villages.

After 1907, the newly added column "Name and address of closest living relative in native country" is important for identifying those who were left behind: sometimes a wife, oftentimes a parent. The "address," however, may simply be the name of the town or village.

When you find your ancestor in the passenger arrival lists, check for other people who may have traveled from the same village. They may be related to your ancestor, and these names may likely turn up in censuses as your ancestor's neighbors or as witnesses on documents.

Sometimes the best information is found at the end of the passenger list. This is where births, deaths, and stowaways are generally listed. Had I not turned to the end of the list, I would have totally missed learning that my great-aunt had given birth at sea. There was no indication on the listing with the rest of the family that this event had occurred.

Two other gems, if extant, that were microfilmed at the end of each passenger list were the "Record of Detained Aliens" and "Record of Aliens Held for Special Inquiry." Many immigrants were detained at Ellis Island and other immigrant receiving stations for a night or two until relatives could come to pick them up. Information on the "Record of Detained Aliens" included the name of the alien, number in the family who were detained, the cause of detention, their disposition (relationship, name, and address of person picking them up), the date and time of release, and the number of meals they ate during detention. Unescorted women and their children were always held until their husbands or other male relatives claimed them. If the male escort was waiting for them when the boat docked, then the woman and her children will not be listed on the record of detained aliens.

On the "Record of Aliens Held for Special Inquiry," the cause of the detention was noted, actions taken by the Board of Special Inquiry, date of hearings, the number of meals eaten during detention, and if deported, the date, name of vessel, and port from which they returned to Italy. The initials "L.P.C." under the cause meant "likely public charge" (a person who probably would not be able to support himself and thus be a burden on public tax dollars); "L.C.D." referred to "likely contagious disease." Both were grounds for deportation. (Deportation records are discussed in more detail later.)

Visas, Passports, and Alien Registrations

Records of the Visa Office contain records from 1910 to 1940. These are located at the National Archives in Washington, DC, and are arranged chronologically in ten-year groupings and then alphabetically. This time span is open for research. Passports were not required of United States citizens who traveled abroad before World War I; however, for added protection, many people obtained them anyway. The jurisdiction fell under the Department of State, and its records were transferred to the National Archives. The passport applications span the period 1791–1925. Those passports less than seventy-five years old are restricted by Privacy Laws and may not be viewed by the public. Applications from 1906 to 1925 include name of applicant, date and place of birth, name and date and place of birth of spouse and children, residence and occupation at time of application, immediate travel plans, physical description, and a photograph. Letters from employers, friends, and relatives may accompany the file.

Aliens were required to register their current addresses and places of employment annually with the federal government under the Alien Registration Act of 1929. These records, which are covered by the Privacy Laws, have limited access through the Freedom of Information Act at the Immigration and Naturalization Service (INS). In order to obtain copies of any Immigration and Naturalization Service record, write to the Historical Reference Library, 425 I Street, N.W., Room 1100A, Washington, DC 20536, and request the address of the INS district office nearest to where the event occurred. For example, if your ancestor was an alien in or near Philadelphia, Pennsylvania, then you would write to that district office of the Immigration and Naturalization Service for alien registration information. Currently, there is no fee to obtain copies of records from the INS; however, if the request is "large or unusual," researchers will be notified in advance of any charges.

Naturalization Records

Prior to 1906 an alien could apply for citizenship at any court of law. An immigrant could file "first papers," or a declaration of intent, at one court and "final papers," or a naturalization petition, at a different court. After 1906 records were forwarded to the Immigration and Naturalization Service, and inquiries should be directed to them (see specifics for ordering INS records under "Visas, Passports, and Alien Registrations"). Some naturalization records have been microfilmed and are available through the Family History Library. In their catalog holdings, check under the state and county in which the naturalization took place.

In the declaration of intention, or "first papers," an alien "renounced allegiance to foreign sovereignties and declared . . . intention to become a U.S. citizen." Proof of United States residence was not required. The records created before 1906 primarily contain the applicant's name, country of birth, date of application, signature, and sometimes the age, occupation, and date and port of arrival. After 1906 the intention includes the applicant's name, age, occupation, and personal description; date and place of birth; citizenship; present address and last foreign address; vessel and port of embarkation; U.S. port and date of arrival; date of application; and signature.

In the naturalization petition, or "second or final papers," an adult immigrant who had already filed the intention papers and had met the residency requirements now made a formal application for citizenship. Information on post-1906 petitions includes name, residence, occupation, date and place of birth, citizenship, and personal description of applicant; date of emigration; ports of embarkation and arrival; marital status; names, dates, places of birth, and residence of applicant's children; date at which U.S. residence commenced; time of residence in state; name changes; and signature. After 1930 photographs may also be included. In the deposition that accompanies the petition, witnesses signed in support of the applicant.

Prior to 1922 wives automatically became citizens when their husbands did.

As of July 17, 1862, an alien twenty-one years or older could acquire citizenship by enlisting in the military and receiving an honorable discharge. The alien did not have to make a declaration of intention, or prove residency. He simply petitioned the United States government.

Two helpful guidebooks on naturalization records are John J. Newman's *American Naturalization Processes and Procedures, 1790–1985,* and Christina K. Schaefer's *Naturalization Records of the United States.*

If you don't know exactly when or where your ancestor arrived, it would be beneficial to seek the naturalization record since, depending on the year, it may give this immigration information, or at the least, narrow the possible time of arrival. Be aware, however, that discrepancies in names of ships and exact dates of arrival are common. If you don't find your ancestor arriving on the date and on the ship cited in a naturalization record, check other ships that arrived the same day from Italy or for the named ship arriving on other days during a given year as listed in the *Morton Allan Directory*.

Deportations

Between 1892 and 1930 more than 134,000 aliens were deported. If an immigrant ancestor has "disappeared" from typical records likes censuses, deportation may be a possibility.

Few foreigners to America were turned away before the late-nineteenth century, but beginning in 1882, a multitude of new laws specified who would be excluded, admitted, or later deported. "Undesirables"—individuals whose known or suspected past included criminal activity, mental health problems or idiocy, and those likely to become a public charge—were denied entrance. By 1917 there were many extensions to the 1882 act—specifically, barring anyone over sixteen years of age who could not read English "or some other language or dialect" and children under sixteen traveling alone, as well as contract laborers and others known or suspected to be professional beggars, prostitutes and their procurers, offenders of moral turpitude, polygamists, anarchists, epileptics, the feeble minded, and those infected with a loathsome or contagious disease or a physical or mental disorder that would prevent them from obtaining work.

New arrivals deemed to be a member of one of these classes were briefly detained at the port, then sent back to the country of origin on the next returning ship of the same line—that is, they were *barred* from entry. Other aliens were admitted but later may have been charged with violation of one or another immigration law; if the charges were proved to the satisfaction of an examining board, they were *deported*. Once an immigrant was admitted, the statute of limitations varied for discovery of a prior transgression or commitment of a new one, depending on the legislative act then in effect. Beginning in 1891 deportation was limited to within one year after the immigrant was admitted. The 1917 act, however, stated that "at any time within five years after entry, any alien who at the time of entry was a member of one or more of the classes excluded by law [or] any alien who shall be found in the United States in violation of this act . . . shall, upon warrant of the Attorney General, be taken into custody and deported." Another act the following year amended this to remove the five-year limitation, stating that "at any time after entering the United States . . ."

Existing records vary according to the situation:

- In open-and-shut cases involving barred aliens, no special records were created. Only a notation was made on the original passenger list next to that alien's name. His or her name was generally added to the supplemental section of the passenger manifest, "Record of Aliens Held for Special Inquiry." When extant, these lists are included on the microfilm of the ship rolls, and appear following the passenger list to which they pertain. Details include the name of the detainee, the cause of detention or rejection, the date and time of discharge or return, the number of meals consumed while detained, and—if the rejected immigrant was waiting for someone— the name and address of the American contact.

- If a case was appealed to the port's Board of Special Inquiry and a hearing file was created, the record of that case will be found in the regional branch of the National Archives that has the records of the port of entry in question (e.g., for extant Board of Special Inquiry records created at the Port of San Francisco, one should check at the National Archives–Pacific Sierra Region).

- For an alien who was admitted but later threatened with deportation after identification as a member of an excluded class, a personal file was created. The U.S. Immigration and Naturalization Service pursued the case amid proceedings that were ruled by the U.S. Supreme Court to be administrative rather than criminal.

Some aliens who were arrested and deemed part of an undesirable class were given a choice: they could voluntarily leave America or be deported. If they left of their own accord and paid for their own trip home or arranged to take a seaman's post to work for their passage, they avoided a record of deportation and could return to America when they no longer belonged to the excluded class. If the government paid travel expenses, however, a deportation record was created; and the deportee was not allowed to return to the United States for at least five years.

Most deportation case files contain the following information:

- The original affidavit of probable cause, filed by an agent of the Department of Justice.
- A carbon copy of the original arrest warrant.
- The record of the preliminary examination given to the alien at the time of arrest.

- A complete official transcript of all the proceedings in the case and of testimonies given in regular hearing(s) conducted by the immigration inspector.
- A summary of findings and recommendations by the Commissioner General of Immigration.
- Actual evidence or record of evidence submitted in the case.
- A record of bail when secured.
- A brief submitted by the alien's attorney.
- Letters submitted by the alien's friends and employers.
- A memorandum from the Secretary of Labor or his representative, giving a final decision on the case—together with instructions for disposition.

Deportation files are extant for the period 1906–57, and are in the custody of the INS. Since the INS in Washington, DC, has a lengthy backlog, contact with a district office will expedite requests. Addresses for district offices may be obtained by writing to the Reference Librarian at the Washington, DC, address cited earlier under "Visas, Passports, and Alien Registrations."

Military Records

Since most southern Italians arrived in America in time for one or both of the world wars, this discussion will focus on those wars. If, however, your ancestors arrived earlier and they likely served in a prior war, consult *U.S. Military Records,* by James C. Neagles, and *Military Service Records: A Select Catalog of National Archives Microfilm Publications* for information on records, indexes, and accessibility.

Draft registrations for World War I were held in 1917 and 1918. Whether a man was an alien or citizen, he was required to register for the draft. On 5 June 1917 all men between the ages of twenty-one and thirty-one years of age were required to register. An act of 5 June 1918 required all men who had become twenty-one years of age since 5 June 1917 to register. A supplemental registration was held 24 August 1918, at which time men who had become twenty-one years old since 5 June 1918 were required to register. Finally, on 12 September 1918, there was a registration of all men between the ages of eighteen and twenty-one, and thirty-one to forty-five years old.

At the National Archives Southeast Region (1557 St. Joseph Ave., East Point, GA 30344), more than 24,000,000 World War I Selective Service records are on file. The Family History Library has these records in their collection. The records are filed by state and draft board. In order to search these records, you need the full name of the person and his city and/or county at the time of registration. If the registrant lived in a major city, as did the majority of Italians, then a street address is also necessary. To locate someone's address during this time period, consult city directories (discussed later).

The records tell the name and address of the applicant, his age and birth date, citizenship, occupation and employer, distinguishing physical marks, and, depending on the form, his place of birth, the name of the closest living relative, and whether the applicant served in a foreign military before coming to America.

The records of the fourth draft registration for World War II are available through regional branches of the National Archives for the states in their jurisdiction. Men born between 28 April 1877 and 16 February 1897, or those between the ages of forty-five and sixty-five years old, were included in this fourth registration.

Italian aliens who resided in the San Francisco Bay area of California were relocated and interned for a brief period during World War II. Primarily these were Italians who had never become United States citizens, even though they may have resided in the United States for half their lives. Records of individual internments are difficult to obtain as, once again, they fall under restricted access of the Privacy Laws. For individual internment records first try writing to the Immigration and Naturalization Service as discussed under "Visas, Passports, and Alien Registrations" earlier in this chapter. Internment camp records and some individual case files may also be found in various record groups at the National Archives in Washington, DC: Record Group 389, Records of the Office of the Provost Marshal General: Records Relating to Prisoners of War, 1941–1956; and Record Group 85, Records of the Immigration and Naturalization Service. For more information, consult Christina K. Schaefer's *Naturalization Records of the United States*.

Newspapers

Newspapers, usually available on microfilm in public libraries serving the area covered by the newspaper, may be accessed through interlibrary loan. They are an excellent source of family and social history, giving accounts from a contemporary viewpoint. Many newspapers are published daily or weekly. Obituaries, marriage and engagement announcements, reports on fifty-year wedding anniversaries, family reunions, 100th birthday celebrations, birth announcements, local news columns, and legal notices will provide information for all family historians.

To locate the whereabouts of out-of-print newspapers, consult *History and Bibliography of American Newspapers, 1690–1820,* by Clarence Brigham, and *American Newspapers, 1821–1936,* by Winifred Gregory. For newspapers still in publication, the *Gale Directory of Publications and Broadcast Media* gives the date the newspaper was established, publishing information, the name of the editor, and an address. Another helpful guide is the Library of Congress' *Newspapers in Microform.* There is a volume and supplements for newspapers in the United States and one for foreign countries (see bibliography). *Newspapers in Microform* gives the names of the libraries that have the newspapers, which will expedite interlibrary loan requests.

Writing letters to the editor or placing advertisements in current newspapers may help you locate distant relatives or your ancestors' former neighbors that may still be living in an area.

If your ancestors were literate in the Italian language (determined by information on passenger lists and censuses), they may have read Italian language newspapers. New arrivals seeking relatives who immigrated before them may have placed an announcement in an Italian language newspaper. These newspapers also reported items typically found in American newspapers, such as obituaries. The largest collection of these papers is found at the Immigration History Research Center in St. Paul, Minnesota (see Appendix B). The Center will interlibrary loan newspapers on microfilm.

City Directories

A city directory is an alphabetical list of inhabitants in a given locality. Though it is a valuable tool to researchers, directories may be frustrating to use since there was no set standard for every city directory. The information contained in directories and their availability varies from city to city and from one time period to another. Most directories were issued annually, but publication may be sporadic for small communities. These books list names of adults, including adult children living with parents. A city directory may also give the person's occupation, name of employer, the person's home address, and spouse's name. Although uncommon, cases where an individual has died, listing the person's date of death, have been found. More commonly, however, the spouse will be listed as a widow the year following a death. In small communities, if the family moved out of the area, directories may tell where the family relocated.

The best place to find city directories is at the local library in the locality of interest. There are also major collections at the Library of Congress in Washington, DC; the Family History Library in Salt Lake City, Utah; the Allen County Public Library in Fort Wayne, Indiana; and the New England Historic Genealogical Society in Boston, to name a few.

A helpful feature of some city directories is the "Householder's Index" or "Criss-Cross Directory." This may be found in the back of the book, or it may be a totally separate volume. Instead of an alphabetical listing of individuals, it is an alphabetical/numerical listing of streets followed by the house numbers and inhabitants. This may be used when researching and reconstructing a neighborhood. Checking the criss-cross directories, and other records for the neighbor of a household near or next to where your ancestor lived may give you a person to contact who might know where your ancestor moved.

City directories are invaluable if you need to know your ancestor's address for World War I draft records or for census records that are unindexed. Immigrants tended to show up in directory listings a year or more after arrival. This may help you estimate when your ancestor came to this country. Once again, be creative with spelling when looking for your ancestor's name. DeBartolo could also be listed as DiBartolo, D'Bartolo or other variations.

Voter Registrations

As a whole, voter registrations will reveal political preferences of Italians in a given area. Individually, they may give clues to citizenship. Prior to 1906, each state had its own residency requirements for aliens governing their eligibility to vote. In the early 1880s, at least eighteen states and territories required that an alien need only file a declaration of intention to have voting privileges. By 1905, only nine states still had these requirements: Arkansas, Indiana, Kansas, Michigan, Missouri, Nebraska, Oregon, Texas, and Wisconsin. Voter registration records may only be extant for the past five to seven years, while some counties may have retained records from the turn of the century. Generally kept at the county level, some states may have statewide lists of voters. Besides checking the county courthouse for voter registrations and indexes, also check state archives, historical societies, and libraries for records that may have been donated and transferred to these repositories.

Social Security Records

The Social Security Master Death Index is available on compact disc at the Family History Library, its family history centers, and many other libraries, and contains lists of deaths reported to the Social Security Administration. The index contains partial files on more than 55 million deceased people who had Social Security numbers and whose deaths were reported to the Social Security Administration. It covers deaths from 1962 to the present, although there may be some records from as early as 1937. The Social Security program began in 1935.

Gaining access to the Social Security Death Index is simple. You do not need to know the person's Social Security number. When information on a person is displayed, it will give the following information for each: date of birth, Social Security number, month and year of death, state where the Social Security number was issued, the last state where the person resided, state where benefits may have been sent, and ZIP codes for the address of residence at death and the address where the benefits were sent.

Once you have your ancestor's Social Security number, by writing directly to the Social Security Administration, Freedom of Information Officer, 4-C-5 Annex Building, 6401 Security Blvd., Baltimore, MD 21235, you may obtain, for a small fee, a photocopy of your ancestor's original Form SS-5, "Application for a Social Security Number Card." This information is available only for deceased people, so it may expedite your request if you include a photocopy of your ancestor's death certificate. Unlike the information found in the Social Security Death Index, the administration records will be more detailed, giving the names of the applicant's parents, date and place of the applicant's birth, the name and address of the employer when the applicant applied, and the applicant's address at the time of application. This was the only American record I found where my great-grandfather, Salvatore Ebetino, himself stated the names of his parents, including his mother's maiden name. His death certificate, where someone else reported the names of his parents, failed to give his mother's maiden name. A good case for leaving no stone unturned!

Cemetery and Mortuary Records

On rare occasions, you may find a village or country of origin carved on your ancestor's tombstone or listed in the funeral home records. Italian Americans frequently imbedded into their loved ones' tombstones a specially prepared tile photograph of the deceased. This may be the only photograph left in existence of an ancestor.

Italian immigrants also preferred to engage the services of a funeral home operated by other Italians since these morticians retained the funeral practices and customs of the Old Country. The funeral home and cemetery may likely be listed on the death certificate, but you can also check city directories for undertakers in your ancestor's neighborhood. Published in even-numbered years is the *American Blue Book of Funeral Directors*. This directory, found in the reference section of many public libraries, is arranged by state, then town/city.

Church Records

While the vast majority of southern Italians were Catholic, some were Jewish and Protestant. When possible, new arrivals preferred to attend a Catholic church with an Italian priest. Once again, city directories may be able to help you pinpoint churches in the Italian neighborhood where your ancestors likely attended.

Any of the church's records—baptism, first communion, confirmation, marriage, or burial—might list your ancestor's native village in Italy. This especially may be the case if there was a significant church population of a particular ethnic group, or if the priest had common origins with the church member. Church records may also give you maiden names of women and help you make connections between relatives.

Catholic church records may be difficult to obtain, however. Some parishes will not allow people to examine the parish records; the priest, if he has time, or the church secretary will check the records for you. There may be a charge to obtain a copy or abstract of the records; if not, offering a donation is wise, especially since you may need a record from that parish again.

Chapter 4
Researching Italian-American
Historical Perspective

Genealogia dice solo metà la storia; storia sociale dice il riposo.

(Genealogy tells only half the story; social history tells the rest.)

or

Ce n'è di più di quanto non salti agli occhi.

(There is more to it than meets the eye.)

Putting your ancestors into historical perspective is an important aspect of your research, not only for writing a family history, but also for getting the most out of your genealogical studies. Learning historical perspective is studying what life was like during your ancestors' day and time. For example, when James Michener writes a historical novel, he must put his characters into historical perspective so that you believe you are reading about a particular time period. What did people do on a daily basis? How did they act? What did they eat? How did they dress? Why did they behave in a certain manner? What were the customs of the time? And so on. You learn about historical perspective and your ancestors' daily lives from reading *social histories.*

Social histories are accounts of the everyday lives of everyday people, as opposed to traditional history textbooks that focus on national events and figures. Studying the social history of Italians will help you to understand what the genealogical records are telling you—or *not* telling you—and why your ancestors behaved in certain ways. Remember in Chapter 1 the discussion about birds of passage? The trend of Italian men commonly going back and forth to Italy a couple times before bringing their families to America, if at all? This is the social history: the typical experience of a group of people. If you were unaware of this common pattern for Italians, you might not think to look for your ancestor on other passenger lists beyond your initial finding.

In another example, you may not know exactly when your Italian ancestor came to America, but knowing the social history—that the peak years of Italian immigration were between 1901 and 1904—could give you a starting point.

Social historians use the same sources genealogists use, only they look at whole communities or segments of the population instead of isolating individuals or specific families. In fact, they may be the ones to uncover new record sources for genealogists. I happened upon a book by historian Stephen Fox called *The Unknown Internment: An Oral History of the Relocation of Italian Americans During World War II*. I was fully aware that in this country, Japanese Americans and some German Americans were relocated and placed in internment camps during World War II; but I did not know, until I found this book, that some Italian Americans were also relocated. Non-naturalized Italian Americans living on the California coast around San Francisco were relocated for a short time period and placed in internment camps. This was an important discovery for me since my great-grandfather never became naturalized and was living in San Francisco during World War II. Was he relocated? Although I haven't found yet that he was, Fox's book led me to the record group of internees in the National Archives. Had I not known about Italian-American relocations, I would never have thought to look for this kind of record. (See discussion under Military Records in Chapter 3: Searching U.S. Sources for Clues Specific to Italian-American Research.)

When our Italian ancestors came to this country, they brought with them their culture, customs, and traditions and adapted them to their new life in America. Even though our families are unique, to an extent, they are also very similar to other Italian families; they have a shared cultural heritage that sets them apart from Polish Americans, German Americans, and Croatian Americans.

Social history research is important for any ethnic group, time period, or class of people. In some cases, there may be gaps in genealogical research that can be supplemented with social history. For example, I don't have any detailed accounts of what it was like for my ancestors to come through Ellis Island, but by researching the typical, common experience, I can supplement what I do know with what other people encountered. When we don't have accounts of activities of our own ancestors, we can speculate on what it was probably like based on the typical experiences of others who did leave accounts of similar activities.

If your ancestors were alive and you were able to do oral history interviews with them, what would you ask them about their lives—besides who were your parents and where did you come from? Think about what you want to know, write down the questions, then research the answers. Let's look at a case example and take the historical perspective research step-by-step.

Case Study of Researching Historical Perspective

Step 1: Formulate Questions

I wanted to know about Antonia Vallarelli's experience of coming to America as a seventeen-year-old girl unescorted by a male in 1914. What was it like for her? Did she travel completely alone or with a female companion? How did she get from landlocked Terlizzi to the port at Naples? Was she detained at Ellis Island? Who picked her up?

Step 2: Re-examine Original Records on the Individual

I re-examined Antonia's passenger arrival list to see if there was any information that would answer these questions, which it did. Though there were no obvious relatives with whom she was traveling, the passenger named after her on the manifest was a twelve-year-old girl, Maria Palmetta, who was also from Terlizzi. The passenger named before Antonia's entry was a twenty-three-year-old housewife, Vincenzia Rutigliano, who last resided in New York, but she named a grandfather in Terlizzi as the nearest relative left behind in the Old Country. None of the people these three ladies were going to join in America or those they'd left behind in Italy bear any obvious connection other than they were all from Terlizzi. Though these three young women have no apparent blood ties, because they were grouped together on the passenger list and all originated from Terlizzi, we can speculate that they likely traveled from Terlizzi to Naples together. Added to this is what we learned in Chapter 1 about nativism and the types of people who were excluded from America: anyone traveling alone under the age of sixteen. Twelve-year-old Maria Palmetta had to be traveling with *someone*, probably Antonia, since Maria was listed *after* Antonia on the manifest. The likelihood of these three women not knowing each other and by chance meeting at the port among thousands of other emigrants is slim.

Then, going to the end of the passenger list, I discovered that Antonia and Maria Palmetta were detained for awhile at Ellis Island. The cause of Antonia's detention was she was waiting on the arrival of her sister Maria Riccio to pick her up. Twelve-year-old Maria's father eventually claimed her.

The passenger list alone, then, answered many of my questions. Almost all, in fact, except for "what was it like?" Antonia was a young woman with no apparent male escort. Was she approached by any men who would have offered to "take care of her" and sold her into white slavery? Was she scared? Lonely? Did she miss her mama? The ship's list doesn't answer these questions. So my next step is to turn to social histories and find out what *other women like Antonia* experienced, so that I can speculate based on their experiences what Antonia's situation may have been like.

Step 3: Research in Social Histories

In order to find social histories, you need to get out of the genealogical library. While you may find a few of these types of books in that department, mostly you will be using public and university libraries. Here are the subjects I looked under in the computer catalogs to answer my questions about Antonia:

- The immigrant experience
- Italian Americans
- Ellis Island

I also checked the same topics in *The Reader's Guide to Periodicals* for articles (remember those fat, green books in the reference section you had to use when you wrote your high school research paper?).

After reading and skimming many books and articles, I found the following sources answered my questions about women like Antonia and what their immigration experience was like:

- "Hope, Tears, and Remembrance," by Edward Oxford, in *American History Illustrated* (October 1990).
- *The Ellis Island Source Book,* by August C. Bolino (Washington, DC: Kensington Historical Press, 1985).
- *Keepers of the Gate: A History of Ellis Island,* by Thomas M. Pitkin (New York: New York University Press, 1975).
- *La Storia: Five Centuries of the Italian American Experience,* by Jerre Mangione and Ben Morreale (New York: HarperCollins, 1992).

- "The Italian Immigrant Women Who Arrived in the United States Before World War I," by Valentine Rossilli Winsey, in *Studies in Italian American Social History*, edited by Francesco Cordasco (Totowa, NJ: Rowman and Littlefield, 1975).

Step 4: Taking Notes

If your goal is to write your family history, then you will need to take notes on the information that deals with your topic of interest. In this case, we're looking at women's immigration experiences and immigration experiences in general. For notetaking, I recommend using index cards, both 3 x 5 and 4 x 6.

The 3 x 5 index card is used as bibliography ("bib") card. For each source you examine, jot down all the bibliographic information on the card in a standard citation, along with the name of the library and call number in case you need to recheck that source:

Bolino, August C. *The Ellis Island Source Book*. Washington, DC:
Kensington Historical Press, 1985.
UCCS Library
E184.I8
S82

Even if your goal right now does not include writing a family history, you may change your mind in the future (maybe after reading this book?), so it's better to take down at least the bibliographic information rather than repeating your search later.

When you do compile your family history, these bib cards can be placed in alphabetical order, then typed into your word processor without any effort.

The 4 x 6 index cards you will use as note cards, taking one note per card:

Bolino, p. 18	women's imm. exp.
Unescorted women were detained until someone picked them up.	
The U.S. gov't didn't want to encourage prostitution or white slave	
trading.	

In the upper left corner, note the author's last name and page number in the text. There is no need to cite the other bibliographic information since that's already on your bib card. In the upper right corner, write the subject you're researching. When you begin writing, you can group the cards together with like subjects. The rest of the card is used to paraphrase or quote from the book. By using handwritten notecards instead of taking notes with a computer, I find I am more likely to paraphrase short segments than quote material. I'd rather not copy a lot of another author's work verbatim and then have to seek permission to use it. When I type notes, it's too quick and too easy to copy too much. By paraphrasing, you can put the author's idea into your own words and then cite your source in your footnotes.

If your goal is simply to learn about the historical perspective to increase your research knowledge, you may not want to take the time now to take notes. The next chapter, Understanding Your Italian-American Ancestors for Research Success, shows you some of the benefits of researching social history.

Chapter 5
Understanding Your Italian-American Ancestors for Research Success

Chi lascia la via vecchia per la nuova,
sa quel che perde e non sa quel che trova.

(Whoever forsakes the old way for the new,
knows what he is losing but not what he will find.)

When Italians came to this country, the vast majority clung to the customs, traditions, and lifestyles known by their families for generations, adapting their culture to their lives in America. Slowly, as the generations became more American than Italian, these folkways diminished and are in danger of disappearing completely. Traces of many folk customs and superstitions may still remain, however, and can aid in your genealogical research.

Learning about Italian-American social history—the patterns, preferences, customs, traditions, and folkways—can actually determine whether your genealogical research will be successful or not. In previous chapters I've shown you how knowing the typical Italian-American immigration pattern could lead you to look further into passenger lists (see "birds of passage" in Chapters 1 and 3). I've also illustrated how social histories can lead you to records you may not have known existed (see Italian-American relocations during World War II in Chapters 3 and 4). Now I'd like you to look at other aspects of social history that might have a bearing on the direction of your genealogical research: work, religion and superstition, family and naming patterns, childrearing and education, foodways, sickness and health, and old age and death.

Work

When they got to America, they learned three things:
that the streets were not paved with gold;
that the streets were not paved at all;
and that they were expected to pave them.

In 1890, Italian Americans were involved in the following occupations:

Laborers	41%
Trade and Transportation	21%
(railroad workers, peddlers, etc.)	
Manufacturing	19%
Farming and Fishing	15%
Professionals	2%

In southern Italy, men were mostly fishermen or *contadini* (peasant farmers) who worked outdoors. When they got to America, the trend was not toward farming and agriculture, although men still preferred outdoor occupations. Primarily, most new arrivals earned a living as unskilled laborers: ragpickers, pick and shovelers, truck farmers, street peddlers, and organ grinders. The more industrious were likely to try self-employment, establishing their own businesses in the food industries: restaurants, delis, groceries, wineries, and pasta factories.

Italian-American women, on the whole, stayed at home with the children. They may have added to the family income, however, by doing factory piece work at home, such as putting together artificial flowers. Single Italian-American women never worked as domestics in someone else's home, as was common for Irish-American women. The Italian culture did not permit a single woman to live outside of her family.

Italian men were interested in making money, with a goal of either returning to Italy and buying land or bringing their family members to America and supporting them when they arrived. Because of this focus on earning an income, Italians as a group were slow to become naturalized citizens of their new homeland, if they became naturalized at all. Taking time off of work to go to a courthouse and fill out papers was simply not a priority to many Italian men. For some, they hadn't planned to live in this country permanently anyway. If you are having difficulty finding naturalization papers for some of your Italian relatives, this could be the reason. It always puzzled me that I could never find a record of my great-grandfather, Albino DeBartolo, becoming a

U.S. citizen. After I learned the social history, it occurred to me that he may never have become a citizen, though I still haven't given up the search.

In fact, Albino used to be a genealogical nightmare until I studied the social history and realized he exhibited several aspects of typical Italian-American behavior. Here's a summary of his activities:

1905–06	lived in Harrison, New York
ca. 1907–08	went back to Italy
1909	came back to America and headed for Harrison again
ca. 1911	returned to Italy
1912	came back to America and headed for Bedford Hills, New York
1913	wife and kids arrived, destination Norwich, Connecticut
1914–15	lived in Worcester, Massachusetts
1916–18	lived in Boston, Massachusetts
by 1920	lived in Manhattan
by 1925	lived in Brooklyn
by 1930s	lived in San Francisco

I just knew the Mafia must have been after him, and that's why he had to keep on the move. Although not nearly as romantic, the real explanation came from the social history research and helped solve some of the mystery. He was a bird of passage who returned to Italy twice before bringing over his family; he had a high mobility rate when he was in America, moving at least every ten years and sometimes more frequently; and he worked as a laborer on the railroad (which also explained his high mobility since he followed the track that was being laid for the New York, New Haven, Hartford Railroad). Either because he was so busy earning a living or he never planned to stay in America, he never bothered to became naturalized.

If I hadn't learned about the high return migration rates of Italians, I would have stopped looking for him on the first passenger list I found for him. If I hadn't learned about the high mobility rate for immigrants, I might have lost him. If I hadn't learned about Italian labor opportunities on the railroad, I may not have tied him in with the railroad since the city directories only listed him as a laborer. (Incidentally, histories and maps of railroad lines were instrumental in confirming his occupation and reasons for moving so frequently.) And finally, if I hadn't learned that some Italians, particularly those who had a high return migration rate and no plans to stay in America, also had a low naturalization rate, then I wouldn't be able to sleep as peacefully at night as I do now knowing that I may never find a naturalization record for him.

Religion and Superstition

Dio in cielo e Papa in terra.

(God reigns in Heaven, and the Pope rules on earth.)

The predominant religion for the majority of southern Italians was Catholicism, although followers of Protestant and Jewish faiths are not uncommon. In Italy and America, most Italian Catholic men did not attend church as regularly as their wives and children. They went on three occasions: when someone was "hatched, matched, or dispatched." Fortunately, these three rites of passage—baptisms, marriages, and burials—created records. Men also attended church on major religious holidays like Christmas, Easter, and the patron saint's feast day celebrated in their community.

Italians primarily enjoyed the Church for its pageantry, spectacle, and the fostering of family celebrations rather than for religious significance. The Church in Italy represented the wealthy landowners and was not considered a source of comfort to the peasant class. When they got to America, the Church was dominated by the Irish who had arrived several decades earlier. Irish Catholics and Italian Catholics had severe differences. Each had its own ideas of observances and the relationship between the priest and the people. The Italians saw the Irish as religious fanatics who put great emphasis on the priest and his ability to serve the community. The Irish thought the Italians ignorant and superstitious because they believed in the evil eye, witches, and wearing amulets of protection like horns (*cornicelli*). The Irish also felt that the Italians placed too much emphasis on saint and Madonna worship.

Despite low church attendance, Italians were very religious. To them, being good or bad, moral and religious—a *cristiano*—had nothing to do with how often one went to church. They preferred to pray to saints and the Madonna, believing that these deities were more approachable than God, and that they empathized with the peasants' struggles. One Italian woman claimed that she only went to church on St. Anthony's Day because he was more powerful than God and performed more miracles. "Besides, he is so handsome." Appeals for help were made to the appropriate saint: St. Biagio for a sore throat, St. Lucia for eye problems, St. Rita for gynecological disorders, St. Rocco for serious diseases, and St. Jude for hopeless situations.

Each village in Italy celebrated its own patron saint with a feast day. This custom was continued once Italians came to America. Though Italian immigrants may have chosen to leave their native village and forget life in the Old Country, they rarely forgot their patron saint. Neapolitans honor St. Gennaro; Sicilians from Palermo worship St. Rossilia; those from the east coast of Sicily pray to St. Agatha. If you do not know where in Italy your ancestor originated, through social history research and oral history interviews you may learn what patron saint day your ancestors may have celebrated. This could lead you to the village of origin.

Family

La Famiglia

Il padrone di casa sono io, chi commanda é mia moglie!

(I am the master of my household,
but it is my wife who commands!)

Throughout Italy's rich history, many different races have invaded and tried to conquer the country. The boot was considered a valuable geographic site. More than a dozen different tribes and nations have invaded, colonized, and enforced their own rule. The peasants of southern Italy have had to endure centuries of exploitation by wealthy landowners and foreign intruders. Because of this, Italian peasants had a great distrust of outsiders, the government, and the Church. The bonds created by the family, which was the only institution they trusted and depended on, enabled them to endure. Their fellow villagers also provided comfort. This attitude followed them to America and was another reason they clustered with relatives and fellow villagers upon arrival in this country. Considering this distrust of outsiders, and especially people working for the government, you can imagine how they viewed the census taker who came knocking at their tenement door. This may explain gross errors and omissions in enumerations for your ancestors.

In Italy and for some first-generation Italian Americans, marriage was by family arrangement. Though love wasn't necessary, it was desirable, and potential partners could object to a match made by two families. Italians of the first two generations in America almost invariably married other Italians. Men preferred marrying someone from their own village and may have even returned to Italy or sent for a bride. The next best match was to marry someone from the same province or a southern Italian region. Rarely did northern and southern Italians marry. Marriage outside of the ethnic group or the Catholic religion was not encouraged. The ideal ages for an Italian bride was eighteen and for a groom, twenty-eight. Witnesses to marriage were usually the groom's brother and the bride's sister, and these two generally became the godparents of the first-born child.

Once the couple was married, the bride and groom adopted traditional gender roles. The husband/father was viewed as the family's ultimate authority. He commanded respect from his wife and children, and was sought after for advice, even though he may have had little interaction with his wife and children otherwise. Remember, he was busy working and trying to support his family. Divorce, separation, and desertion were rare among Italian Americans.

Women were to emulate the Madonna and to nurture, care for, and serve their families. A married woman was to be asexual in public and not attract the attention of other men. Intimate matters such as aspects of sex and reproduction were handed down verbally from mother to daughter. Premarital sex dishonored the family. Although not unheard of, of all the immigrant groups, Italians were the least likely to have children out of wedlock.

Babies were typically born at home with the aid of an Italian midwife. The mother could give birth to a child in the middle of the night but was expected to prepare breakfast for her family the following morning. She returned to her daily activities not because she felt ready, but because she had to. Immigrant women in general had a greater chance of dying in childbirth than American women, and Italian women had a higher death rate from pregnancy than any other ethnic group. And, of Italian women, Sicilians had an even higher death rate among pregnant women. The causes have been attributed to frequent pregnancies, inadequate diet and medical care, and unsanitary conditions during the childbirth.

To limit family size, birth control and self-inflicted or aided abortions were available and more common than we might think today. It was not considered a moral issue for these women, but an economic one. A large family in Italy was needed to work the fields and produce an income. In America, an already large family, crowded into a two-room tenement apartment, that continued to add more mouths to feed was not practical. In addition, nativists, who feared over-population among these "swarthy, papist newcomers," encouraged Italians and other immigrant groups to control their family size through the use of contraceptives like the rhythm method, condoms, and diaphragms. Italians were more likely than other Catholic ethnic groups to use methods other than the Church-accepted rhythm method. Therefore, unexplained gaps between the births of children could be a result of family limitation—not necessarily that a child was born and died or that the father was away.

The traditional naming pattern common among Italians can be found in the first couple of generations in America:

First son after father's father
Second son after mother's father
Third son after father
First daughter after father's mother
Second daughter after mother's mother
Third daughter after the mother

Use of necronyms—the custom of naming the next born child after a deceased baby—was also common. Because names were chosen to honor the older generations, if a child died bearing a relative's name, it was given to the child who was born next, usually regardless of sex. The baby was simply given the masculine or feminine version of the name.

Let's take a look at the Ebetino family:

Children of Salvatore and Angelina (Vallarelli) Ebetino

Francesco, b. 21 Nov. 1900, Terlizzi, Bari, Italy.
Fortunato, b. 14 Nov. 1902, Terlizzi, Bari, Italy; died 14 Nov. 1902.
Fortunato, b. 25 Feb. 1904, Terlizzi, Bari, Italy.
Stella, b. 27/28 May 1905, Terlizzi, Bari, Italy.
Isabella, b. 17 Dec. 1910, Rye, Westchester County, NY.
Felice, b. 8 Apr. 1912, Rye, Westchester County, NY.
Michele, b. 12 Feb. 1914, Rye, Westchester County, NY; died between 10 May 1914 and 12 Apr. 1915.
Michele, b. 12 Apr. 1915, Rye, Westchester County, NY.
Salvatore, b. 4 Apr. 1917, Rye, Westchester County, NY.

Even if we didn't know the names of Salvatore and Angelina's parents, we can surmise them based on the naming pattern. The first born son, Francesco, should be named for Salvatore's father, which, further research revealed, he was. The second son, Fortunato, was indeed named for Angelina's father. But he died; so the child born next, who happened to be another boy, became grandfather Fortunato's namesake. The next child is a female, and she is indeed named for Salvatore's mother. Isabella carries her maternal grandmother's name. Here is where the naming pattern deviates. The third son and daughter should traditionally be named after the parents, but they were not. Felice and Michele were the names of Angelina's brothers. Once again, the use of a necronym is seen when the first Michele died. The fourth son and last child was named after his father.

Notice, too, the five-and-a-half-year gap between Stella's and Isabella's births. Further research revealed that Salvatore left his family and immigrated to America, leaving Italy in April 1906. It is certainly possible that he left Angelina pregnant and the next child did not survive. Angelina and her surviving three children—Francesco, Fortunato, and Stella—arrived in America on 18 February 1910. After being reunited with her husband, ten months later she gave birth to Isabella.

Childrearing and Education

L'educazione dei figli si deve incominciare nelle braccia della sua madre.

(A child's education ought to begin in his mother's arms.)

Italian Americans have always insisted that their children be well educated (*ben educato*). Well educated to them, however, did not mean attending public or private schools. It meant being raised with proper values, attitudes, and skills that benefited the family. By 1877 in Italy, there was compulsory education for children ages six through nine, but this was not enforced. The ability to read and write was useless to the peasant society. To them, formal education meant only two things: paying more taxes and destroying the unity of the family.

Work provided sufficient moral training for offspring, and social and cultural values were taught at home. Children were required to help contribute to the household purse. In America, unmarried daughters who did not work outside the home in factories were still not encouraged to attend school since they were needed at home by their mothers to help care for the smaller children. Many children who were sent to school, stayed only until the minimum legal age when they could drop out.

"Only a fool makes his children different or better than himself," stated one Italian proverb. In the public schools, teachers taught American traditions and values, ignoring Italian values. As one man later put it, "We were becoming Americans by learning how to be ashamed of our parents." The American school system emphasized the importance of the individual and productivity; whereas, the Italian's values revolved around what was good for the family.

Because of this distrust of the school system and the belief that their family and work provided all the education a child needed, Italian Americans had a high rate of truancy, absences, and disciplinary actions. For the genealogist who is able to locate school records, these may provide a unique insight into their ancestor's character.

Parochial schools were also undesirable because they were run mostly by Irish nuns and priests. If Italians sent children to school at all, the public school was the lesser of the two evils. They certainly did not want their children becoming "Irish."

Foodways

Questo è motivo di riflessione.

(That's food for thought.)

Do you know of any Italian family where food is unimportant? Unheard of! A good Italian wife always asked visitors, "Did you eat?" Food was a crucial element both in family celebrations and daily life. Eating meals together was the center of Italian family life. As the generations pass, Italian Americans may accept more and more of "American" ways, but their preference for certain foods remains the same. Food habits are more resistant to change than other aspects of a person's life. This was one area, too, where the newly arrived Italians could maintain their ethnic identity without receiving negative reactions, since practically everyone enjoyed Italian food. Food was a production and cooperative effort of the family: bought with the money earned by the father and prepared with love by the mother. The sharing of food was an act of hospitality, and refusing food was an insult.

Italian regional food differences are actually becoming more pronounced, as we see by a sampling of titles of current cookbooks: *The Good Food of Italy, Region by Region; Regional Italian Cooking; Southern Italian Cooking*.

So how will researching your ancestor's food preferences help you in your genealogical research? Along with adding a rich cultural aspect to your family history, knowing what your antecedents ate in America may help you determine the region in Italy from where your ancestors came. For example, in Apulia where my ancestors originated, their primary protein dish was fish; eel in particular was a delicacy for this region. Garlic played a secondary role in their cooking; onions were preferred. When I interviewed my grandmother's cousins, they told me about how they always ate eel on Christmas Eve after they immigrated to America. And, according to a 9 August 1993 article in *Newsweek*, "Do Our Genes Determine which Foods We Should Eat?" our own nutritional needs may be based more on what our ancestors ate than what we eat today.

Wine was considered a food and drunk only with the meal. Even children as young as two years old were given watered-down wine. Because drinking was done in the context of the family meal, Italians had a low rate of alcohol abuse, not to mention that drunkenness was viewed as a condition of unmanliness.

Sickness and Health

Dopo la quarantina, un male ogni mattina.

(When forty years you attain,
every morning brings an ache and pain.)

Generally, Italian Americans tend to have a lower rate of psychiatric hospitalization than any other ethnic group because of their tendency to turn to the family for support. When there is a breakdown in the family system, then there is an increase in emotional problems. And, as we've seen with their distrust of outsiders, the first generation or two were reluctant to seek outside medical care.

Italian Americans also seem to have a lower threshold of pain than other groups, and are more symptomatic and complain more. They have more gastrointestinal ailments and are more preoccupied with getting some relief and forgetting about their suffering. Those who have kept to a traditional Italian diet—low in animal fats, high in vegetable oils, and daily consumption of red wine—have a low rate of heart disease. Leading causes of death for the immigrant generation and their children in the peak years were more likely from diseases of bacterial origin.

As with most cultures, until scientific cures became prevalent, folk remedies were popular among Italian Americans. There were several remedies for a cold. One was to drink a wine toddy by boiling red wine and adding cinnamon sticks, cloves, sugar, and a cut-up orange, including the rind. To prevent a sore throat, a person was to wear garlic around the neck (naturally, an uninfected person would come nowhere near the person with the garlic necklace, which reduced the exposure to germs!). Garlic was also used to remedy high blood pressure, rheumatism, and bronchitis. Applied to a child's navel, garlic also relieved the afflicted of worms. Chamomile tea cured indigestion in children, served as a relaxant, and relieved menstrual cramps.

There are several inherited diseases to which Italian Americans are prone. One is thalassemia, also known as Mediterranean Anemia or Cooley's Anemia, and is a trait that occurs when a person inherits one thalassemia gene from only one parent. A person with the trait is well and usually unaware of having the condition. Some people with the thalassemia trait have a mild anemia, but this generally does not cause symptoms. If one parent has the thalassemia trait and the other doesn't, there is a 50 percent chance with each pregnancy that the baby will be born with the thalassemia trait. If both parents have the thalassemia trait, there is a 25 percent chance with each pregnancy that the baby will have thalassemia major.

Someone with thalassemia major inherits two thalassemia genes, one from each parent. This is a severe disease due to a deficiency of hemoglobin (red blood cells). The baby appears normal at birth, but toward the end of the first year, appetite and energy diminish. The skin becomes pale, certain bones of the face may become prominent, and growth is slower than normal. Blood transfusions are required and are generally continued throughout the person's life. There is no cure, and normal life span is shortened.

To be tested for thalassemia, request it specifically when you have blood drawn.

Two other genetic diseases you may want to research in your family are sickle cell anemia and Glucose-6-Phosphate Dehydrogenase (G-6-PD) Deficiency, or Favism. Sickle cell anemia, considered more common among black Americans, may also find victims among people from Greece, Italy, southern Turkey, and several Mid-Eastern populations. This inherited condition is caused by a changed hemoglobin called hemoglobin S (S stands for sickle). Usually, red blood cells are round; however, if there is a lot of hemoglobin S in the red blood cells, when they lose oxygen, they may become pointed or "sickle" shaped. G-6-PD Deficiency, also known as Favism, becomes apparent after the afflicted person eats fava beans or inhales fava bean pollen. The person develops hemolytic anemia and jaundice. Favisim is more prevalent among males who originate from Asia and Mediterranean countries like Greece, Italy, and Israel.

With so many genealogists interested in genetics and medical history, this topic would be an interesting and informative one to explore during an oral history interview. Perhaps some of the home remedies are still used in your family. Knowing your family's health history can also help you predict potential problems for future generations.

Old Age and Death

Si parla bene del morto.

(Speak only good of the dead.)

As parents aged, they expected their children to take care of them. Italian-American daughters, rather than sons, generally housed aged parents. This is a reversal of the custom in rural Italy where the eldest son, even after marriage and starting a family of his own, continued to live in the father's household. Italian Americans rarely used nursing homes; if they did, the preference was for one with Italian-speaking personnel or one sponsored by the Catholic Church.

The father was the head of the family (*capo della famiglia*) until he died. A married son did not become head of a family, even his own, until the father's death, even if he resided in a separate household.

When someone died, a funeral mass took place after the body had been waked for forty-eight hours. The wake generally took place in the home. Shades were closed, mirrors were covered, and clocks might be stopped at the hour of death. Friends and relatives paid their respects to the deceased's family. The immediate family was expected to be in attendance and remain with the body around the clock. And there was always plenty of food and wine.

The undertaker was chosen with great care. If possible, he was someone from the same region in Italy as the deceased or one who would cater to the traditional customs associated with death. Even the monument maker might have Italian origins. Italian tombstones and monuments were often elaborate sculptures of saints, the Madonna, or of the deceased. Italian Americans also commonly incorporated tile photographs into the tombstone, with faces of the deceased set so that they somehow always seem to look directly into the eyes of anyone who looks into theirs. Italian Americans were also likely to be buried in a Catholic or Italian cemetery.

Once again, Albino DeBartolo serves as a good example (I just love this guy!). He died in San Francisco in the 1940s. The mortuary that handled the arrangements was Valente, Marini, and Perata Funeral Home. His memorial marker was made by L. Bocci and Sons. Albino was buried in Italian Cemetery in Colma, a suburb of San Francisco. Even the attorney who handled his probate was Italian: Julian Pardini.

Of course, for genealogists, all Italian businesses dealing with death should be checked first. Information on funeral home and place of burial may come from the death certificate. Some of the people who handled various aspects of the funeral may still be in business. One Italian stonecarver found in the San Francisco Yellow Pages boasts being the fifth generation of stonecarvers. That's more than 150 years of potential records.

There may be other aspects of social history (language dialects, dress, housing, leisure activities) that may also interest you or that may relate specifically to your family. Explore these and see how they help in your genealogical research. The social history aspects presented here are the most common ones and given as examples of how researching historical perspective will guide your research understanding.

Chapter 6
Using Italian Records in America

Come mi fa ottiene in Italia da qui?

(How do I get to Italy from here?)

Writing to Italy for Records

One way of getting records from Italy is by writing for them. I have had great luck in writing for and obtaining birth, marriage, and death records from everyone else's ancestral village but my own family's. But be prepared for a wait. The Italian postal system is very slow. Your letter should be written in Italian and should include two postal international reply coupons and a money order for about $5 per record. I've never had any problem using U.S. postal money orders.

If you aren't fluent in Italian, there are a couple ways to have your letter translated. First, look in your local phone book for a school or college where Italian is taught. In Colorado Springs, for example, there is a Foreign Language Center that will translate letters for a fee. Or there may be a student willing to do it.

Second, you can copy one of the many form letters available in how-to books like Trafford Cole's *Italian Genealogical Records*.

Third, you may want to try one of the computer programs that do translations, like MicroTac Software's "Italian Assistant." The only problem with the software translation is that you need to use formal English. Slang does not translate well. The real beauty of the software is that if you receive a reply from someone in Italian, you can retype or scan in the letter, and the software will also translate from Italian to English.

Finally, you may want to try to find a distant relative from your ancestor's native village who may be willing to help you. The Family History Library (discussed in more detail later) has phone books from many cities in Italy. The only problem is that most of them date from 1980. You may purchase your own phone book from any city in Italy by calling AT&T at 1-800-432-6600 or 1-888-582-3688. The operator will give you a price and take credit card orders. To pay by check or money order, send the appropriate fee with your request to Lucent Technologies, Commercial Sales, P.O. Box 19901, Indianapolis, IN 46219.

For my ancestor's little village in Italy—Terlizzi—I wrote to a dozen or so DeBartolos listed in the phone book. I received only one reply, and he referred me to a DeBartolo in Florida!

Hiring a Researcher in Italy

Another way to get records from Italy is to hire a researcher there. Researchers for hire may be found through advertisements in magazines like the *Genealogical Helper, Heritage Quest*, and *POINTers* (Pursuing Our Italian Names Together—see Appendix C for more information). Hourly rates vary, and you will also be paying expenses (transportation, lodging, and maybe food), since rarely will you be lucky enough to find a researcher living in the village your ancestors came from. I highly recommend reading Trafford Cole's book, *Italian Genealogical Records*, before hiring someone, however, so that you will be an informed client. He gives an excellent account of what records are available and their accessibility.

Italian Records on Microfilm in America

While you would no doubt enjoy making a trip to Italy to research your family history, it may not be necessary. Even if you were planning a research trip, why waste valuable time there viewing records that you could have looked at before you left? Instead, spend the time researching records you can't get anywhere else.

The Church of Jesus Christ of Latter-day Saints (Mormons) established the Family History Library in Salt Lake City, Utah, in 1894, to gather records that would help people trace their heritage. Since then, the Library has earned the reputation of having the world's largest collection of records. Through its microfilm and book collections, researchers can search records from throughout the world. For example, the library has about 450,000 rolls of film from more than 2,000 archives, county courthouses, and other repositories in the United States, including 80,000 rolls of federal sources. For Italy, there are more than 10,000 rolls of microfilm.

The book collection contains more than 225,000 volumes of local histories, published genealogies and family histories, periodicals, and other research aids.

While a majority of the Library's holdings pre-date the 1900s, there are many records available for the late nineteenth and early twentieth centuries, the time when most Italians came to America. Examples include a statewide death index for California, 1905–1990; United States city directories, 1901–1935 (with more being added each year); World War I draft records; Veteran's Administration pension payment cards, 1907–1933; and New York City birth certificate index, 1881–1965.

The Family History Library is open six days a week and is open to the public. There is no charge to use the Library and its resources in Salt Lake City. For a free copy of the booklet "A Guide to Research in the Genealogical Library," write to the Family History Library, 35 North West Temple Street, Salt Lake City, Utah 84150.

In 1964, the Library established family history centers so that people would have more access to the records. There are now more than 1,800 centers that operate in fifty-five countries. By writing to the Family History Library in Salt Lake City, you can obtain a list of worldwide center locations. Through a family history center, researchers may rent for a small fee almost anything available on microfilm or microfiche in Salt Lake. Rolls of microfilms may be rented for three weeks, six months, or placed on indefinite loan, but the rolls remain at the center where researchers may view the film anytime the center is open.

The International Genealogical Index (IGI) is a 200 million-name index arranged by localities and lists dates and places of births, christenings, and marriages. It is continually updated with thousands of new names added each year. Through this index, a reference number is provided so researchers can locate the record from which the information was supplied. Always check for your surnames in this database, keeping in mind that this is an *index*, not a *source*. You need to go beyond the IGI and find the record from which the information was taken.

The Family History Library Catalog is the "card" catalog of the entire holdings. The catalog is on CD-ROM and microfiche and lists microfilm, microfiche, and published resources. The microfiche catalog is divided into categories by locality, author, title, subject, or surname. The computerized version may be searched by locality or surname only, but it is usually updated more frequently than the microfiche catalog. This catalog is what you will check in order to determine if your ancestral village in Italy has had it records microfilmed.

Most of the Italian records on microfilm come from the *Ufficio dello stato civile,* or civil registration office of a village. Colletta's *Finding Italian Roots* and Cole's *Italian Genealogical Records* give examples of the civil records along with English translations. Not every village has been microfilmed, but the Family History Library staff is still filming as many records and time periods as the *stato civile* will allow. Most civil registration records—births, marriages, and deaths—have been microfilmed from 1809 to 1865. Some village officials allowed microfilming of their records into the early 1900s. To illustrate how varied the microfilm coverage is, here are a few examples: Terlizzi, 1809–1865; Villa Rossi, 1810–1910; and Verona, 1630–1871. In some areas, church records may have also been microfilmed. The years on film for some church records in Tornia, for example, cover 1823 to 1899; for Marco, 1666–1923; and for Marzano, 1575–1950 (so why couldn't *my* ancestors come from Marzano?).

Keep in mind that the civil records are written in Italian, the church records in Latin. But even if you have limited knowledge of Italian, I doubt you will have any trouble with the civil registration records. It will quicken your search if you memorize names of the months (*gennaio, febbraio, marzo, aprile, màggio, giugno, lùglio, agosto, settèmbre, ottobre, novèmbre,* and *dicèmbre*), days of the week (*doménica, lunedì, martedì, mercoledì, giovedì, venerdì, sàbato*), and cardinal and ordinal numerals. Or take along an Italian-English dictionary that has a table of these items. Many numbers, such as the year, are written out instead of using numerals; e.g., *L'anno mille ottocento ventuno,* instead of "in the year 1821."

One little word you need to watch for that can make a difference in your research is the word *fu.* It means "the late." It will precede someone's name; e.g., *fu Michele,* meaning *the late Michele.* This will help you approximate the year of death for someone if you find Michele recorded as living in one record and listed as "the late" in a later record.

Another key word, found in some marriage records, is *maggiora* or *maggiore,* which means the eldest surviving son or daughter. This will clue you that you may have the first born child of a couple. You should still check for births four or five years prior to a couple's marriage, however. Illegitimacy was not uncommon among Italian peasants. Or, the first child may have died in infancy.

An Italian genealogical key-word list is available for purchase from the Family History Library. Check with your family history center librarian to order one, or write directly to the Family History Library, 35 North West Temple St., Salt Lake City, UT 84150 (801-531-2331).

The civil registration records usually have one volume per year and most have indexes—filmed usually at the beginning of the volume, but some appear at the end. If there is no index, it usually isn't too time consuming to search page-by-page. Look to see where the subject's name is recorded on each document (the name of the deceased on a death record, for example) and check that spot for each record. Some of the records and indexes have water damage or have been worm-eaten and may cause difficulty in reading the records. (Here's a treat that will make your research more interesting: traces of the little worm carcasses can even be seen on the microfilm!)

Also, if you plan a trip to the Family History Library in Salt Lake City, write ahead and request that the village's microfilm collection be available to you. In some cases, the films are kept in storage since there may not be sufficient demand for these films to be kept readily available on the European floor of the Library.

These films may also be rented through your family history center. But make sure your center has a microfilm reader with at least a 42 power magnification lens. The Italian records were filmed on 16mm film and are nearly impossible to read without high magnification.

The beauty of Italian civil registration records is that you can reconstruct whole families since most families lived in the same village for generations. Here is an example of three generations compiled solely from birth, marriage, and death records on microfilm from Terlizzi:

1. FELICE VALLARELLI was born about 1800–02, in Terlizzi, Bari, Italy, the son of Michele Vallarelli and Maria Nicola Ziccolella. Felice died between 1865 and 1870, probably in Terlizzi.

He married LUCIA RUTA, who was born about 1803–05 in Terlizzi, the daughter of Michele Ruta and Arcangela deLeo. She died probably after 1865 in Terlizzi.

Children, all born in Terlizzi, Bari, Italy:

2.   i. MICHELE, b. 14 Oct 1831; m. 2 May 1858 to Palma Rosa Mangiutordi.
3.   ii. GIUSEPPE ANTONIO, b. 6 Mar 1834; d. 24 Nov 1858, no issue.
4.   iii. MARIA NICOLA, b. 22 Feb 1836; m. 8 Apr 1860 to Francesco de Manna.

5.   iv. GIOACCHINO, b. 21 Feb 1838; m. Anna — , 18 Oct
     [after 1865].
6.   v. ARCHANGELA RAFFAELLA, b. 17 Aug 1840; d. 20
     Aug 1840.
7.   vi. ARCHANGELO RAFFAELLE, b. 20 Jan 1842.
8.   vii. FORTUNATO, b. 6 Jan 1845; m. 30 Apr 1870 to
     Isabella Veneto.
9.   viii. PIETRO, b. 26 Jan 1849; d. 14 Mar 1849.

Notice that some of the dates given in this example pre- or
post-date the microfilmed records for Terlizzi, which span 1809
to 1865. The birth years given for the parents, Felice and Lucia,
are estimated from their children's birth records, which recorded
the parents' ages when the child was born. The children's birth
records also list that Felice and Lucia are natives of Terlizzi.
Felice's date of death was calculated as between 1865, when the
last year of death records was microfilmed, and by 1870 when
he was recorded as *"fu* Felice" on his son's marriage record.

Now I know what you're thinking. How did I get a marriage
record from 1870 if the microfilmed collection stopped at 1865?
A friend who also has ancestry from the same village as mine
was kind enough to abstract some records for me, and this was
one of them.

A bonus on some of the Italian civil birth documents is a record
of the child's marriage when he or she came of age. This was the
case for Gioacchino. His marriage to Anna was recorded on his
birth record. Unfortunately, the handwriting was difficult to read,
so I could not decipher Anna's surname or the year they married. I do know it was after 1865, however, because I could not
find a record of the marriage in the microfilmed records up to
that date.

Another nice aspect of Italian birth records is that they give
not only the parents' names but also the grandparents' names;
thus, we not only know who they were, but we can see whether
the naming pattern was followed. Also note the use of a
necronym and the change from feminine to masculine form:
Archangela Raffaella and Archangelo Raffaelle.

As discussed under passenger arrival records in the previous
chapter, women in legal documents were recorded with their
maiden names. When you search for a death record for any of
your female ancestors, you will be looking for her under her
maiden name, not her married name.

The disappointing part of working with the civil registration
records, however, is the gap left by many of the records that have
not yet been filmed after 1865. Since most southern Italians came

to America between 1880 and 1920, you may find that you are missing one or two important generations that you need in order to connect to your family in the Italian records. This is when you will need to either write for the records, hire someone, or find someone who is going to or who lives in Italy who can close this gap for you.

Chapter 7
Learning About Italy

No, non leggo italiano!

(No, I don't read Italian!)

J ust as you learned about Italians in America through social histories, in order to complete the picture of what life was like in the Old Country, you need to research life in Italy. If you have done the research yourself in microfilmed records from Italy, then you probably have come to realize that the civil records (births, marriages, and deaths) have not told you much about your ancestors' lives. Unlike the multitude of record groups you've been used to consulting in America (censuses, passenger lists, immigration records), unless you visit Italy or hire someone there, you will probably need information to supplement what you find in the civil vital records. Social histories will provide you with the material you need to fill out the gaps in your narrative family history. (For examples, see Chapter 9: Blending Social and Family History to Write a Narrative; and Appendix A: An Example of an Italian-American Narrative Family History.)

Most Italian-American social histories also contain background information on conditions and lifestyles in Italy. General histories of Italy, like Denis Mack Smith's classic *Italy: A Modern History*, deal with the political and governmental points of view, although some social history is included. Trafford Cole's *Italian Genealogical Records* also gives a good overview of Italian history with a slant toward genealogists, but once again he says little about what daily life was like for the peasant class. An excellent demographic and cultural study is Rudolph M. Bell's *Fate and Honor, Family and Village: Demographic and Cultural Change in Rural Italy since 1800*. You may also find some other monographs, like Ann Cornelisen's *Women of the Shadows: A Study of the Wives and Mothers of Southern Italy*, that are particularly helpful.

Two other sources are articles and dissertations written about peasant life in southern Italy. Ask the university reference librarian to assist you, or write to one of the repositories listed in Appendix B and ask specifically if the collection contains anything about your ancestral village or region.

Maps and Atlases

To locate the province and region for some of the smallest Italian villages, the *Rand McNally Road Atlas of Italy* may be your best source. You can purchase this atlas at your local bookstore, or you should be able to order a copy through them. If you're an AAA member, you can pick up free maps and travel guidebooks of Italy from one of their offices. Your travel agent may also be able to get maps or travel posters for you.

Local and Regional Histories

For local and regional histories, try the Family History Library and university libraries. Keep in mind, however, that these histories likely will be written in Italian—a problem for those of us who aren't fluent in the language. Two sources—both written in English—that I have found to be most helpful for regional histories are travel guidebooks and cookbooks.

Travel books, besides having maps, generally give a brief historical overview of an area since antiquity, along with a geographic description. These are abundantly available in bookstores (new and used) and libraries. Books dealing specifically with southern Italy will be more detailed for the regions and some small villages than one about the entire country.

In the same genre as travel guidebooks are books written about other people's travels in Italy. Some that I have found particularly helpful are Carlo Levi's *Christ Stopped at Eboli*, William J. Bonville's *Sicilian Walks: Exploring the History and Culture of the Two Sicilies*, and Barbara Grizzuti Harrison's *Italian Days*. Keep in mind that even though these writers toured Italy in the last ten to fifty years—long after your ancestors left the country— the peasant class of southern Italy has remained virtually unchanged for many generations. These books, and others, will give you a good flavor for life in southern Italy.

Many of the regional Italian cookbooks and books on Italian winemaking contain not only information about Italian eating patterns and customs, but they may also contain historical and local history details. Waverly Root's *The Food of Italy* is one of these books. In fact, I wouldn't really classify it as cookbook, even though that's where I found it in the bookstore. It's more of a regional food history.

Another out-of-the-ordinary cookbook is Helen Barolini's *Festa: Recipes and Recollections of Italian Holidays.* This book gives recipes for religious holidays and many saints' days and discusses the customs and celebrations surrounding each festivity. Carol Field's *Celebrating Italy* is another cookbook with this type of slant.

Even some of the more traditional Italian cookbooks add history, culture, and customs. They are an important source to add to your Italian historical perspective.

Chapter 8
Writing Mechanics and Style Choices

Scrivere la storia di Sua antenato.

(Writing your ancestor's story.)

There comes a point in researching your family history when you must turn off the microfilm reader and decide to start writing. This may feel overwhelming at first; in fact, you may have been putting it off, thinking, "I'll just look at one more group of records, then I'll start writing." Well, let me tell you something: There will always be another record. You need to get to the point where you feel you have covered all the basic records an ancestor could have created in his or her lifetime, then start writing.

Some researchers never get to the point of writing the family history, thinking they'll just leave all the research for someone else to compile and write. Frankly, if you're the one doing the research, it makes more sense for you to write the story. Even if you never take it as far as actually publishing it, when you leave a written account of your ancestors it is less likely to get pitched out with all the charts after you're long gone. Let's face it: names and dates on charts are boring.

Writing a book does feel overwhelming, at first, especially if you don't feel you are a writer. If that's what's stopping you, then take a creative writing course at a community college—or hire an editor to polish your writing. Remember, your family history doesn't have to be a Pulitzer Prize winner. The point is to leave a written account of your ancestry for future descendants. You don't have to be an accomplished writer.

Are You Writing Fiction or Fact?

One of the first questions you have to ask yourself is what kind of a book you plan to write—a fictional account based on your research, or a nonfiction, factual story? Alex Haley's *Roots* is an example of a fictional story based on his ancestry. Gay Talese's *Unto the Sons* is a creative nonfiction story about his heritage that reads like a novel. The example of a family history narrative in Appendix A of this book is also a nonfiction story, but the nonfiction writing style is more traditional than the creative nonfiction approach.

Let's look at the same paragraph written in these three different styles.

Fictional Family History

Deep in his heart he knew he was leaving his homeland, never to return. His home for the next two weeks was an overcrowded ship, below the waterline, in an unventilated, semi-dark compartment. He thought about what awaited him when he arrived. What if the officials in America determined that he wasn't fit to live in this new country? His wife warned him that he was taking a risk.

"Salvatore," she said, "I don't know about this. Our life here is good."

"But it could be better, Angelina. Albino wrote to me and told me of all the opportunities in America."

Salvatore Ebetino was willing to take the risk so that his family would have a better way of life.

In this example, there are a couple of writing techniques telling us that we are reading fiction. The opening sentence, beginning, "Deep in his heart he knew," is the first part to make us wonder if this is a factual account. The start of the sentence, "He thought . . . " adds to the suspicion. Unless Salvatore has personally told us in an interview that "he knew" or "he thought" something, we cannot possibly know it as fact.

The other clue that we're reading fiction is the dialogue. Unless the conversation was recalled during an oral history interview, we can't know for certain that Salvatore and Angelina uttered these words.

Creative Nonfiction Family History

He was leaving his homeland, never to return. His home for the next two weeks was an overcrowded ship, below the waterline, in an unventilated, semi-dark compartment. What would await him when he arrived? What if the officials in America determined that he wasn't fit to live in this new country? This was the risk Salvatore Ebetino was willing to take for his family to have a better way of life.

This example, on the other hand, has no dialogue and no insight into Salvatore's thoughts or feelings. Everything is factual, only written creatively. Nothing can be disputed. He *was* leaving his homeland. He never returned. He *did* live for two weeks on an overcrowded ship. He had no way of knowing what awaited him when he arrived. There was *always* the possibility an immigrant could be rejected. He *was* taking a risk.

Traditional Family History

Salvatore Ebetino left his homeland, never to return. Like thousands of other Italians, he was immigrating to America. He left Italy in 1906 on the ship *Italia*. For the next two weeks, Salvatore traveled in an overcrowded ship, below the waterline, in an unventilated, semi-dark compartment.

You may feel most comfortable with this last writing style. It's more to the point and leaves no doubt that you are writing nonfiction. Of course, adding footnotes or endnotes gives the final confirmation that this is nonfiction.

Find a style that suits you and emulate it. The genre you decide upon is totally up to you and your writing ability; just be sure to make it clear to your readers in an introduction whether you are writing fact or fiction; and if you are writing fact that reads like a novel, make that clear, too. If you prefer to write historical fiction, I recommend you read standard writing guidebooks such as Robin Hemley's *Turning Life into Fiction* and Rhona Martin's *Writing Historical Fiction*.

For the purpose of this book, however, I am assuming you want to write either traditional or creative nonfiction—narrative, factual stories about your ancestors' lives. For other examples, look at Gay Talese's *Unto the Sons*, Ian Frazier's *Family*, or some of the others listed in the bibliography (Also see Appendix A: An Example of an Italian-American Family History Narrative). There are also several writing guidebooks on creative nonfiction writing included in the bibliography, like Jon Franklin's *Writing for Story: Craft Secrets of Dramatic Nonfiction*, and Gay Talese and Barbara Lounsberry's *Writing Creative Nonfiction: The Literature of Reality*.

Determining the Purpose and Scope

Before you begin writing, think about the purpose and scope of your book. Why are you writing it and what will you cover?

Purpose

- Is your goal to document as many generations as possible?

- Do you want to show your readers what life was like for your ancestors in Italy and in America?

- Is the purpose to bring "flesh to the bones" instead of recording just names and dates?

Scope

- Will this be an "all my ancestors" book, covering as many generations as possible?

- Will the main focus be on the immigrant generation, with genealogical summaries of subsequent generations?

- How many generations do you plan to cover in the book?

- Do you want to write short biographies on everyone included in the book?

- Will you interweave one generation into the next in a story format?

Write down your book's purpose and post it next to your computer. This will help keep you focused as you write. I'm in the process of writing a nonfiction story about four generations of the Vallarelli family. Here is the purpose and scope of that book:

> This study features four generations of the Vallarelli family as illustrative of the typical southern Italian and Italian-American experience. It will span two generations of family in Italy and two generations in America. This genealogical, social, and cultural account will not only document the Vallarelli family, but it will also demonstrate the typical, everyday lifestyles and experiences of the southern Italian peasant family in Italy and America, ca. 1800–1930.

Viewpoint

After you've determined your purpose and scope, then you need to think about some other writing mechanics, like viewpoint. Viewpoint determines who is telling the story and which verb tense you will use. Are you going to write the story using first person narrative: *I* did this and *I* found them in this record? Personally, I don't recommend it. The *I*s become overwhelming for the reader unless you are an accomplished writer. The best viewpoint in writing a story about your ancestors—be it fiction or nonfiction—is to use third person narrative: *he* did this; *she* arrived in America, etc., with you as the narrator. This viewpoint is also more true to life. As the narrator, you do not state any information you cannot possibly know, like someone's thoughts. In real life, we don't know a person's thoughts. And you certainly do not want to interrupt the story with your own thoughts. Put those in a footnote. (For more information on footnotes, see Chapter 9.)

History happened in the past, so it's best to write about it in the past tense. Then you don't have to worry about shifting verb tenses.

Characterization

No longer are your ancestors going to be names on a chart. When you begin writing your family history, they become *characters* in a story. But you're not *creating* characters out of your imagination. You have real life people to work with. Characters should be revealed to your reader bit by bit, not all at once as in most family histories:

> Felice Vallarelli was born on 28 March 1880 in
> Terlizzi, Bari, Italy.

Yawn. When we meet someone in real life, no one stands there and reads us life statistics. Why should we meet your ancestors that way? Reveal your characters slowly—through their actions, how they dress, their beliefs, and so on. Let's look at an example from Gay Talese's *Unto the Sons*:

> Ippolita Talese had an aura of mystery about her that often puzzled her grandson, a detachment that sometimes made Joseph ill at ease in her presence; and yet he was oddly pleased that she was his grandmother. He was impressed by her. He was impressed by her well-groomed appearance, her delicate face and fair skin, which was remarkably unwrinkled for a woman of her age, and he was impressed with the fact that she changed her dress each evening before supper, or, at the very least, came to the table wearing a beautiful lace collar, and always emitted a slight but pleasant fragrance of perfume.

> She held her slim shoulders back when she walked, and sat upright during dinner in one of the high-backed chairs that had cushions and were much more comfortable than the furniture that Joseph was accustomed to at home. . . .

Do you get the impression that Ippolita was an extremely proud and meticulous woman? Yet the author never comes right out and *tells* us, "Ippolita was an extremely proud and meticulous woman." He *shows* us through her actions, her body language, and her appearance.

This is an area where oral history interviewing is crucial. While you may be able to show readers your parents, grandparents, and perhaps great-grandparents from your own memories, you will need to get information on some of your ancestors from the oldest generation still living. Talk to these people about their memories of their parents, grandparents, and maybe great-grandparents.

Below are items that reveal character and for you to keep in mind when you write about your ancestors:

- Actions and behaviors
- Clothing
- Speech
- Likes and dislikes
- Friends
- Beliefs
- Food preferences
- Habits
- Body language

Even if you plan to include photographs of your ancestors, describe the picture for your readers. They may not notice certain details, and in the process you are revealing a person's character. The clothing the person is wearing in the photo, for example, can tell social status, the time period, and perhaps an occupation. How the clothing is worn can tell us whether the person is meticulous or careless. It *shows* us aspects of an ancestor's personality.

If you don't have a photograph of your ancestor, and you don't know what he or she looked like, then research how others in the same time and place would have dressed and tell the reader that. What type of clothing did people of that day wear? Did the men wear beards or mustaches? How did women wear their hair?

Character is also revealed through words or dialogue. But as a creative nonfiction writer, you have to be extremely careful with dialogue. You are not *creating* dialogue and putting words in your ancestors' mouths that they may never have spoken. If you are writing about your parents or grandparents or someone whom you knew personally and you are recreating conversations, then using dialogue is appropriate. Or, if you are interviewing your grandmother and she tells about a conversation she had with her grandmother, then this is also appropriate. This is how Gay Talese is able to use dialogue in *Unto the Sons*. But if you are writing about your eighteenth-century Italian ancestor, who died long before anyone living has memory of him, then it's better to stay away from dialogue. It will do nothing but cast doubt as to whether the story is really nonfiction.

Characters should also draw the reader's sympathy. In short, your ancestors were human with faults and failings. The reader wants to see these because, since we are not perfect, we cannot relate to a perfect person. If you were to write, "Rosa was a saint, perfect in every way. Everyone loved Mama Rosa," not only does it make us gag, but we won't believe you. *Everyone* has faults— even Mama Rosa. We need a character/ancestor we can relate to. Now if you were to write, "Rosa was a saint. Everyone loved Mama Rosa. In fact, they loved her so much that no one had the heart to tell her that her spaghetti sauce was terrible." Ah! Now we have a fault, a failing. She's human after all. The woman can't make good sauce. I can relate to that!

You also want to give your characters/ancestors motivation. Your readers have a right to understand why an ancestor acted in a certain way. Remember Albino DeBartolo, the bird of passage who went back and forth from Italy to America? *Why* did he do that? Well, you and I know why because we've learned the social history and this was typical behavior. Now tell your reader. Your readers cannot be expected to know even half as much as you do about the family or social history. *You* are the authority here.

If you're having problems isolating aspects of characteristics for your ancestors, try making a character outline for each one and refer to it as you write your story. On a sheet of paper, fill in as much as you know from your genealogical research and oral history interviews:

Character Outline for Salvatore Ebetino

Name: Salvatore Ebetino
Nickname: "Jack"
Lifespan: 1875–1957
Parents' Names: Francesco and Stella (Tangara) Ebetino

Ethnic Origin: south Italian
Physical Appearance: 5'5", dark complexion, about 162 pounds, black hair, brown eyes, scar on forehead over right eye
Profession: in Italy, *contadino*; in America, gardener
Education: unknown
Economic Status: in Italy, poor; in America, lower middle class
Religious Affiliation: Catholic
Marital Status: married (once) to Angelina Vallarelli
Hobbies: unknown
Health Status: developed diabetes in old age
Cause of Death: pneumonia at the age of 82
Habits/Quirks: smoked imported Italian cigars which he cut in half, smoking each half to within an inch.
Favorite Foods: unknown
Positive Traits: frugal, loved to tell stories
Negative Traits: unknown
Pets: dog named Prince

Salvatore's character description came from his death certificate, naturalization records, passenger arrival list, and oral history. Some other genealogical sources that may reveal character are newspaper articles and obituaries, court records, pension applications, draft registrations, diaries, letters, photographs, wills, and probate inventories.

Setting the Time and Place

The next aspect of writing your ancestor's story is going to be in describing settings: You will need to know well the period and place in order to describe for your reader the time and season, the interior and exterior designs of homes and buildings, the type of furniture and objects found in an ancestor's home, the town and community, and the geographical appearance of the locality.

Try to avoid setting the time period by merely stating the date, "The year was 1920." Instead, *show* us 1920. Your readers may have little knowledge of what 1920 looks like. You show the time period and setting by describing the form of lighting people used, the types of furniture, the modes of transportation. Here again, try not to overwhelm your readers with description; give it to them little by little. When you visit New York City, you don't have a bird's eye view. You see it bit by bit. Your family history is not a geography lesson. Give us specifics, not abstracts. Don't write,

"The street was lined with trees." Tell us what kind of trees: oaks, maples, aspens, evergreens, etc. Readers want to be able to visualize in their minds the time and place.

If the story revolves around a setting where you have never been, research it. Interview someone who has been there; read travel books. You don't have to break your arm to know it hurts. Likewise, you don't have to visit Italy to be able to describe the countryside for your reader. And, I can safely say, you will *never* experience traveling aboard a crowded ship in steerage for two weeks during the 1880s. But you can research what it was like from others who did make the passage. People read to experience things they never experienced before.

Some sources that reveal time periods and setting are photographs, probate inventories, Sandborn Fire Insurance and bird's eye-view maps, city directories, topographical maps, land records, tax records, social histories, travel guides, and books on historic homes and antiques.

Bringing Your Narrative to Life

Another aspect to consider is to incorporate in your writing the five senses: sight, sound, taste, touch, and smell. Think of the characters, time period, and setting in terms of how it looks, sounds, tastes, and smells. Most writers concentrate too much on how things look and virtually ignore the other senses. Think about your surroundings right now. What do you hear? What can you see? Are there any smells? Are you eating or drinking something, and how does it taste? How do items in the room feel? Ask these questions when you write about your ancestor's setting.

Here again, go into some detail. Don't just say, "It was raining." What does rain sound like? What would it sound like aboard ship if you were in steerage? On deck? Is it a heavy rain or a drizzle? Details like this will bring life to your story.

Finding the Plot

In order for your family history to be a story at all, it must have a beginning, a middle, and an end; it must have a plot. Something has to happen. This is the action or the events in a story. It's what takes the reader and characters from one point to the next. The plot doesn't have to be a can't-put-it-down thriller á la

Stephen King. It can be as simple as Salvatore Ebetino deciding to leave Italy and starting life afresh with his family in America. The interesting part is in telling the readers about the obstacles that may get in Salvatore's way. How will he pay for his passage and for his family's? Will he pass the exams at Ellis Island or be rejected and deported? Will he be able to find work once he gets to America? Where will his family live?

It doesn't even have to be a success story, either. In fact, tragedies usually have a more lasting impact on the reader. The important part is to develop the conflicts and lead the readers to the resolutions. The beauty of writing about real people like your ancestors is *you know* how the story ends, assuming you've done quite a bit of genealogical research, of course. You know your ancestors left Italy. You know they had to travel by ship to get here. You know they did okay for themselves (or maybe they didn't) once they got here. You know the beginning and the end of your ancestor's story. Now fill in the middle, and tell your readers *why* everything happened the way it did.

Adding Suspense, Humor, Emotion, and Romance

The best-loved stories are ones that make us laugh and/or cry. If you can add suspense, humor, emotion, and romance to your family history, then do so. It will make it more enjoyable to read. Once again, you're not making up stories or fictionalizing. You are *looking* for aspects of your ancestor's life that lend themselves to bringing out the suspense, humor, emotion, and romance that everyone experiences in a lifetime.

The best places for suspense are in the first and last paragraphs of each chapter. This is what keeps readers reading, the need to know what's going to happen next. Again, we're not talking Stephen King-type suspense. But you do need to grab the reader's attention and keep it. Starting off with "Isabella Ebetino was born on 17 December 1910" is going to put anyone to sleep, even another genealogist. You *don't have* to begin your family history with the day your ancestor was born! Start with the most exciting or interesting moment in your ancestor's life. Then "flashback" and pick up the details that led up to this point.

> All of the family gathered at the graveside for seven-year-old Isabella Ebetino's burial. Aunts, uncles, cousins—all came to mourn the tragedy that occurred that hot August day.

Now that the scene is set, go back and tell us how we got to this point.

> Everyone heard the screams coming from the kitchen. From everywhere, people came running. Little Isabella, dancing and playing in the kitchen, did not notice that her mother had set a huge boiling vat of tomato sauce on the floor to cool. Isabella tripped. She fell against the hot caldron, burning her delicate skin.

Leave us hanging—keep us reading—but then tell us what happened next.

Humor may be tricky to add because what sounds funny may not read funny. Make sure you have several people read the humorous parts to make sure you are getting your point across.

Humor can come from oral histories, letters, diaries, newspaper articles, family stories, court records.

Don't be afraid to add emotion and romance. If you have family stories, letters, diaries, or anything that reveals human emotion and romantic feelings, use them in your narrative. If you don't, then research how other people felt about certain experiences or how other people courted and married their spouse. Then you can make a statement like, "Though it is not known how Salvatore met and married Angelina, many Italian marriages were prearranged."

Bringing Your Story to a Close

Finally, don't forget to draw a conclusion to your story. Summarize the highlights of a person's life in a couple paragraphs to end your story. Even if it isn't a success story, try to end on an upbeat note.

> While many Italian immigrants who settled in urban areas were not as fortunate as Salvatore and Angelina Ebetino, those who chose to settle in smaller communities seem to have prospered more. They started out poor, but they adapted and adjusted well to life in their new homeland called America.

Your family history may never be a *New York Times* Best Seller like Gay Talese's; but the point is to get *something* written. After all, you've spent years and countless hours doing the research. Don't leave it unfinished. Pull it all together into a legacy that will be treasured by your family. Tell your ancestors' stories.

Chapter 9
Blending Social and Family History
Research to Write a Narrative

*Quelli che manca di scrivere delle vite di loro antenati merita li è
dimenticati.*

(Those who fail to write about their ancestors' lives deserve to be
forgotten themselves.)

You are in a unique position. You have a chance to make a
real contribution to the field of genealogy, to Italian-
American culture, and to your descendants! Do you realize that? Because so few family histories have been published
about Italian Americans, your book will be among the first. What
will make it valuable to all Italian Americans is that you will be
including social history instead of making it a "names and dates"
book. After all, isn't that what made history boring in high
school? Learning all those dry names and dates and facts? Don't
you think a family history could have the same potential?

Before you get to the point of writing a narrative, you should
have accomplished the following:

- Conducted thorough genealogical research on your ancestors, attempting to check for every possible record created
  during a person's lifetime.
- Conducted thorough social history research, so that you are
  extremely familiar with the time period and the experiences of everyday people in your ancestor's society.

You should have also thought about

- Whether your book will be fact or fiction
- What the purpose and scope will be
- What viewpoint your book will have

- How you can best reveal your ancestors through characterization
- How you can best reveal the time period and setting
- What the plots and subplots are
- Ways to bring your story to life by adding suspense, humor, and emotions

Basically, there are going to be two sections to your family history book:

1. The narrative account of your ancestors' lives

2. The genealogical summary

Preparing to Write the Narrative

Before you sit down at the keyboard and begin writing your family history, it's a good idea to read how other writers have written narratives on their ancestors. Each author has his or her own style and format for writing family history. Read several and emulate the style you like best. Of course, of particular interest to Italian Americans is Gay Talese's *Unto the Sons,* which I've mentioned in previous chapters. Though Talese does not footnote or cite his sources, he has written a factual story about his heritage. The genealogical community, if that is to be your main audience, however, will expect you to document your work and to cite where each piece of genealogical and historical information came from. Other narratives, dealing with non-Italian families, may be found in the bibliography of this book. Some may be out of print, but you should be able to get them through your library, or you may find them in a used bookstore.

You may also want to practice writing your narrative and incorporating historical perspective by composing a few paragraphs placing *yourself* into the historical context. You only need to consult one source and then combine it with your life. Obtain through interlibrary loan a newspaper from your hometown on a significant day in your life in that community, like your wedding day or the day you graduated from high school. Then write a summary of what life was like on that day using the articles and advertisements. Now include your memories of life during that time. Make sure you also draw a conclusion to your summary. Tell the reader why something was popular or why a national event had an impact on your life. You cannot assume your readers will reach the conclusion you want them to; you need to tell them.

And make sure you make appropriate connections and relationships. Here's an example from someone's family history about life after the Depression:

> When I was twelve, we moved into a larger two-story home. That was the year I painted houses. I learned to use a clutch, shift gears, and the other basics of driving a car . . . At fourteen I was a licensed driver . . . and drove through Georgia and up the coast, through the Holland Tunnel, to New York City, and up Fifth Avenue. Here I saw my one and only professional boxing match; Joe Lewis defeated Max Schmeling in Yankee Stadium with a knockout in 2 minutes and 40 seconds of the first round. The Depression was over.

Do you see a problem here? This paragraph is beautifully written until that last deadly sentence. It makes it sound like *because* Joe Lewis defeated Max Schmeling in Yankee Stadium the Depression ended. If the author had concluded by saying, "The Depression was over, making it financially possible for me to travel across the country and see Joe Lewis defeat Max Schmeling. . . . " then we would have a logical connection. Just throwing in a major historical event is out of place and awkward.

Organizing Your Research Materials

When you begin writing your Italian family history, I promise you won't finish it during one rainy Saturday afternoon. No doubt it has taken you years to do all the research. The writing part, I hope, won't take that long, but it will occupy your time for several weeks or a couple of months, depending on how proficient a writer you are.

Your writing area needs to have enough space to allow you to have all of your research notes and documents within handy reach. This area should also be a place that will be relatively undisturbed until the book is finished, so that you won't have to put things away at the end of each writing session.

I have found that writing comes easier if I have all my "tools" within handy reach: a standard dictionary and an Italian-English dictionary, a thesaurus, a grammar handbook, my research notes, post-it notes, paper clips, calculator, pens, pencils, highlighters, chocolate, a cup of tea, my cat in my lap, and a photograph of Michelangelo's David by my computer so that I have something pleasant to look at when I need a break. These are, of course, just the essentials.

Remember how you took your historical perspective research notes on notecards? Now's the time to get them organized. Because you dutifully recorded in the upper right corner the subject each note dealt with, you can now arrange the cards into like subjects in the order in which you want to discuss each topic in the book. Chronological order is probably still the best way for family history writing. So, for example, the cards dealing with life in Italy would begin the narration, followed by the journey to America, followed by settling in America, followed by finding work, followed by bringing the family over. Unless, of course, you are going to add some suspense by starting the story with the most exciting part of your ancestor's life then flash back. In that case, your notecards can easily be arranged to accommodate this.

Summarize the Social History Research

Probably the easiest way to blend your family and social history research is to write the social history first, then insert specific details about your ancestors. Remember back in Chapter 4, Researching Italian-American Historical Perspective, we were dealing with Antonia Vallarelli and what it was like for her to venture to America as an unescorted seventeen-year-old girl? From the social history research I did in the sources I mentioned in that chapter, I wrote the following summation about the typical immigration experience for women:

> Many women who arrived during the peak years of immigration between 1901 and 1914 came alone or with small children. Husbands had arrived in America several years earlier and saved for their wives' and children's passage. Three to five years later, the husband would send for his family and perhaps an unmarried sister. The wife was left with the responsibility of selling any furniture or possessions, getting the necessary travel documents and tickets, and finding a way to the port city. The majority of these women had never even ventured beyond their native villages. And they certainly never had to encounter government bureaucrats. In fact, some women were forced to submit to a demand for sexual favors before they would be given the required documents. They also had to be on their guard against white slave traders or procurers of prostitutes. Upon arrival at Ellis Island, unescorted women were

detained until someone arrived to pick them up. This was the United States government's way of guarding against prostitution or white slave trading. If the woman was single, and a man claiming her stated he was her fiancé, then often the wedding took place right on the Island.

Now, let's insert specific information on Antonia that we know from the genealogical research. I've italicized the changes.

Blending Family History with Social History

Many women, *like Antonia Vallarelli*, who arrived during the peak years of immigration between 1901 and 1914, came alone or with small children. Husbands had arrived in America several years earlier and saved for their wives' and children's passage. Three to five years later, the husband would send for his family and perhaps an unmarried sister. *One of Antonia's brothers, who was already in America, likely helped pay for her passage and encouraged her to come to America. She was single and seventeen when she left Italy in 1914.* Women were left with the responsibility of selling any furniture or possessions, getting the necessary travel documents and tickets, and finding a way to the port city. *Antonia,* and the majority of these women, had *probably* never even ventured beyond *her* native village. And *she* certainly never *would have* had to encounter government bureaucrats. In fact, some women were forced to submit to a demand for sexual favors before they would be given the required documents. They also had to be on their guard against white slave traders or procurers of prostitutes. Upon arrival at Ellis Island, unescorted women *like Antonia* were detained until someone arrived to pick them up. *Antonia was held until her sister Maria Riccio claimed her.* This was the United States government's way of guarding against prostitution or white slave trading. If the woman was single, and a man claiming her stated he was her fiancé, then often the wedding took place right on the Island.

In many cases, you will be speculating on your ancestors' experiences based on the typical experiences of others like your ancestor. You clue your reader by the wording you choose. Words and phrases like

- probably
- like others
- likely

- presumably
- possibly
- plausible
- likelihood
- feasible

clearly indicate that you do not have documents to support your statements; but you do have your research in historical studies that is credible and supports your speculation. It is important, of course, to make it apparent which is the known, specific information on your ancestors and which is the history that may apply to your ancestor. You don't need to interrupt the narrative to give us your source, though. You don't need to say, "According to this historian. . . ." Make your historical transitions smooth using discussion of the same subject matter, then distinguish between the two types of information in your footnotes or endnotes.

Citing Your Sources

Footnotes (remember these from the days before word processors automatically formatted them for us?) are source citations at the bottom of the page; whereas, endnotes are grouped at the end of a chapter or at the back of the book. Whichever you use is up to you and what your word processing software will handle. Regardless, a family history without proper documentation is taboo, whether you're writing it just for the family or for a wider audience. After all, you want to be proud of your work, and show everyone—even family members—the amount of research that went into it.

In a narrative family history, you may choose to cite each piece of data within a paragraph, which gets unwieldy and is cumbersome for your reader, or you can use one note per paragraph, *as long as it is clear to your readers which piece of information came from which source.* Generally, you cite the source in the order in which it was discussed in the paragraph. In the case of the historical information, the general experience may be repeated in several sources.

Now let's look at the same paragraph with one footnote:

Many women, like Antonia Vallarelli, who arrived during the peak years of immigration between 1901 and 1914, came alone or with small children. Husbands had arrived in America several years earlier and saved for their wives' and children's passage. Three to five years later, the husband would send for his family and perhaps an unmarried sister. One of Antonia's brothers, who was already in America, likely helped pay for her passage and encouraged her to come to America. She was single and seventeen when she left Italy in 1914. Women were left with the responsibility of selling any furniture or possessions, getting the necessary travel documents and tickets, and finding a way to the port city. Antonia, and the majority of these women, had probably never even ventured beyond her native village. And she certainly never would have had to encounter government bureaucrats. In fact, some women were forced to submit to a demand for sexual favors before they would be given the required documents. They also had to be on their guard against white slave traders or procurers of prostitutes. Upon arrival at Ellis Island, unescorted women like Antonia were detained until someone arrived to pick them up. Antonia was held until her sister Maria Riccio claimed her. This was the United States government's way of guarding against prostitution or white slave trading. If the woman was single, and a man claiming her stated he was her fiancé, then oftentimes the wedding took place right on the Island.[1]

If you are giving information on an ancestor that came from more than one genealogical document, then you can still use the one note per paragraph style by stating, "Information on Antonia's birth came from her birth certificate . . . ; information on her arrival in America came from her passenger list . . . ; information on her death came from the funeral record. . . . " Make sure, of course, that your genealogical citations are complete, listing the type of record, the date of the record, who the record pertains to, and the repository where the record can be found. Likewise, if you had a quote in the paragraph, you may simply state, "Quote came from . . . " or "The first quote came from . . . , the second quote came from . . . "

---

[1] Specific information about Antonia Vallarelli came from the passenger arrival list of the *Sant' Anna*, sailing from Naples on 29 May 1914, arriving at New York on 12 June 1914, group 5, line 28, National Archives Microcopy T715, roll 2333, volume 5344. Historical information came from August C. Bolino, *The Ellis Island Source Book* (Washington, DC: Kensington Historical Press, 1985), p. 18; Thomas M. Pitkin, *Keepers of the Gate: A History of Ellis Island* (New York: New York University Press, 1975), p. 67; and Jerre Mangione and Ben Morreale, *La Storia: Five Centuries of the Italian American Experience* (New York: HarperCollins, 1992), pp. 92–93.

Blending Oral and Social History

Now let's see how you can blend details from an oral history interview with your social history research. Apply the same principal of writing the social history, then insert information from the interview. Make it a single, flowing narrative by discussing the same subject matter. If you analyze the paragraph carefully, by the wording alone, you should be able to tell what details pertain specifically to the Vallarelli family and what information is about Italian Americans in general. Be conscious of this as you blend your family data with social history.

Meals were an important aspect of Italian-American life, and the Vallarelli family household was no different. Family life revolved around the dinner table for two reasons. First, food to the Italian was a symbol of life; it was the product of the father's labor prepared by the mother. To Italian Americans, "meals were a 'communion' of the family." To waste food was a sin and to refuse food from an Italian hostess was an insult. Rosa Vallarelli always asked anyone who came to her home, "Did you eat?"; then she would offer them food. Another reason family life revolved around the Italian dinner table was that this was the one time during the day when the whole family was, and was expected to be, together. Isabel, Rosa's daughter, recalled that dinner time was practically the only time she saw her father.[1]

Wine, considered a food, was served at most Italian-American lunch and dinner tables and was given in small quantities to children age two and older. The Vallarelli family also had this custom. *Un giorno senza vino é come un giorno senza sole.* (A day without wine is like a day without sunshine.) Rosa's husband, Felice, made his own dark red wine. He made routine trips with his brother-in-law Michael Albanese to the Bronx where they bought grapes. The wine press and barrels were stored in the Vallarelli's household cellar. Wine was never

---

[1]All specific information pertaining to the Vallarelli family was obtained from an oral history interview between the author and Isabel Vallarelli on 27 April 1993. The interview was conducted in Isabel's home at 29 First Avenue, Harrison, Westchester County, NY, when she was 76 years old. Isabel is the daughter of Felice and Rosa (Albanese) Vallarelli. General information on Italian Americans came from Richard Gambino, *Blood of My Blood; The Dilemma of the Italian Americans* (New York: Doubleday, 1974), p. 17; and Frances Malpezzi and William Clements, *Italian-American Folklore* (Little Rock: August House Publishers, 1992), p. 224.

drunk apart from a meal, and despite their wine consumption, alcoholism was rare among Italians since drunkenness was a sign of unmanliness.[2]

Supplementing and Augmenting Italian Records

Suppose you have been able to research your family in the microfilmed records. You may have been able to reconstruct a whole family like the one in Chapter 6. Beyond the bare-boned vital information (birth, marriage, and death dates), you likely also noted occupations listed in these records. If they were typical southern Italians, some of them were *contadini*. Researching that aspect, you may be able to write a summary of life and combine it with your family history research:

> The Vallarelli family had a long history of peasant life. Accessible birth, marriage, and death records from Terlizzi, Bari, Italy, document that Felice and Lucia (Ruta) Vallarelli, as of the 1830s, were *contadini* (peasant farmers) and remained so throughout their lifetimes. These small landholders, who generally lived in villages like Terlizzi, rented land from absentee landlords. Most *contadini* had a one- to three-hour walk to the fields each morning and evening from their homes. By 1806 many European peasants were emancipated from feudal control, but the peasantry in Italy were still bonded and offered *contadini* like the Vallarellis few opportunities to rise socially or economically. If anything, life was getting more grueling. As governments became stronger, they targeted the peasant class for more taxes and to fill military quotas. In response, "peasants tenaciously maintained old loyalties to their region, their priests, [and] their habitual ways. Often they developed elaborate ties of family."[1]

---

[2] Gambino, pp. 25–26, 222; Malpezzi and Clements, pp. 235–36.

[1] By "accessible birth, marriage, and death records," I mean those records available on microfilm from the Family History Library in Salt Lake City. For Terlizzi, the vital records span 1809 to 1865, although they are not inclusive for each event. For example, the birth records start with 1817; death records are available for 1809, then there is an eight-year gap with no available death records until 1817; marriage records begin with 1824. In the birth records for all of the children of Felice and Lucia (Ruta) Vallarelli, spanning 1831–49, Felice was listed as a *contadino*, and Lucia as a *contadina*. General historical information came from Mortimer Chambers, et al., *The Western Experience*, 5th ed. (New York: McGraw-Hill, 1991), pp. 926–28, Map A-25 in the Cartographic Essay; quote from p. 926.

Or, let's suppose you just want to summarize a common aspect of daily life in Italy during the nineteenth century, but you have no documents confirming or supporting your family's involvement. Again, write the social history, and incorporate your family in a sentence or two:

> Surviving everyday life was a challenge in itself for *contadini* like the Vallarellis. Along with natural disasters such as earthquakes, droughts, and flooding, nineteenth-century peasant families also had to deal with frequent outbreaks of smallpox, meningitis, typhoid, cholera, and malaria. Brought to the South by invading troops, who peasants referred to as the "spreaders of the cholera dust," cholera killed thousands of people annually. The disease was characterized by diarrhea, vomiting, muscle cramps, dehydration, and collapse. Malaria was a constant plague since ancient times, but spread more rapidly in the mid-1800s when deforestation caused "soil from the hills [to deposit] in the valleys, choked their drainage, and formed swamps in which malaria mosquitoes bred." The malarial infection had an incubation period of about ten to thirty-five days and gave the victim chills, fever, and sweating.[1]

Even though I don't know for a fact that the Vallarelli family was plagued with these epidemics, I can still include them in my narrative about the common experience for southern Italians.

Genealogical Analysis and Summary

After the narrative portion of your family history book, you may want to include a genealogical analysis and summary of families or a drop-line descendancy chart. Since we don't want to interrupt the flow of a narrative story to discuss the probability of what record is likely to be more correct over another one or which pieces of evidence led us to which conclusions, that information can preface the genealogical summary of a couple and their children. It is here where you can discuss all your problems with the research and how you solved them. Or you can include

---

[1] Denis Mack Smith, *Italy: A Modern History* (Ann Arbor: The University of Michigan Press, 1959, 1969), pp. 150 and 258; *The Merck Manual*, 13th ed. (Rahway, NJ: Merck Sharp and Dohme, 1977), pp. 94–95 and 159–60. Quote from Phyllis H. Williams, *South Italian Folkways in Europe and America* (New Haven: Yale University Press, 1938), p. 3.

the analysis in the footnotes of your story. A genealogical summary looks like the one in Chapter 6 dealing with the Vallarelli family. The summary is the bare bones information, giving the facts of births, marriages, and deaths, and any other specific information that pertains to the family that you could not work into your narrative.

The genealogical analysis and summary are really an appendix, although some of my colleagues will cringe when they read this. To them, this is *the* most important part, the reason for *being* a genealogist, and the only recognized format for writing family history. There's no question that it has its place. If you were going to write your family history for a genealogical journal, then the analysis and summary are the meat and potatoes. But that's not the only way to write family history. If you want your family history to be *read* and *savored* by family and non-genealogists, then the story is the dessert, which, everyone knows is the best part and should really be eaten first. Of course, it is helpful to your readers to include the analysis, summary, and descendancy chart so they can quickly see how people are related and how you reached your conclusions. These are important elements in your family history. In fact, I wouldn't do a book without an analysis and summary. But they are only *part* of the book.

There are two accepted numbering systems for genealogical summaries: the Register System (based on the format used in *The New England Historical and Genealogical Register*) and the NGSQ (based on the format used by the *National Genealogical Society Quarterly*). For more details on these numbering systems and their intricacies, please read Joan Ferris Curran's "Numbering Your Genealogy: Sound and Simple Systems," in the *National Genealogical Society Quarterly* 79 (September 1991): 183–93. Make sure you include an introduction to your book that clearly explains the numbering system you chose.

Chapter 10
Publishing and Distributing Your
Italian-American Family History

Roma non fu fatta in un giorno.

(Rome was not built in a day.)

You've done a lot of work. I heard someone once equate researching, documenting, and writing your family history as the equivalent of doing a doctoral dissertation. By now, you probably have no doubts that this statement is true.

After you have written a draft of your family history to your satisfaction, let it get "cold" while you have other people read it. Put the manuscript aside for several weeks and then come back to it and make revisions. But don't think you'll be able to goof off and take a vacation during this time. There's still lots to do and think about.

Copyeditors and Proofreaders

Have several people read and comment on your draft manuscript before you publish. If possible look for people who can offer different perspectives:

- Someone who knows the family and will spot any relationship problems or name misspellings.

- Someone who knows nothing about genealogy who will be honest and tell you if the story is interesting and whether the numbering system was easy to follow.

- Another genealogist who will pick up on any problems with the numbering system or faulty genealogical analysis.

- A historian who will spot any inaccuracies in your historical perspective.

- Someone with editing/proofreading background who will catch grammar and punctuation errors.

If you personally don't know people with all these qualifications, then you may have to hire a professional editor/proofreader, historian, etc. Check the Association of Professional Genealogists Directory at your genealogical library or order a copy from APG, 3421 M Street, N.W., Suite 236, Washington, DC 20007. The cost at this writing is $15.

Illustrations

While your manuscript draft is being read by others for comments, this is a good time to decide what to include as illustrations. Here is a list of items you may want to consider:

- Maps of Italy, the ancestral village, the American neighborhood
- Photographs of ancestors, ships, localities, tombstones, artifacts
- Genealogical documents
- Genealogical charts

Self or Commercial Publishing

Most family histories are self-published; you pay for everything. There are many publishing houses that deal specifically with short-run copies of books. First, check your local Yellow Pages to see if there are any in your area. Then, look at magazines like the *Genealogical Helper* for advertisements of small-press publishers. Elizabeth Petty Bentley's *Genealogist's Address Book* also lists family history publishers. Two extremely helpful articles dealing with self-publishing are "Preparing Manuscripts for Offset Printing" and "Publishing Genealogical Research: Commercially and Privately." Both of these articles were written by Ann Hege Hughes, president of Gateway Press, a genealogical self-publishing firm in Baltimore. The articles were published in the *Association of Professional Genealogists Quarterly* (see the bibliography under writing and publishing guides). If your genealogical library does not have copies of this journal, then write to APG (listed earlier) for a back issue or reprint of the articles.

Contact several self-publishing companies. They will send you a form to complete, asking you for specific information about your book like number of pages and illustrations, then they will give you a price quote. Ask for not only a quote on the whole print run, but also a per book cost so you know how much to charge. While it's doubtful you'll make a profit, do add in your costs, like shipping, the cost to cover the number of copies you will be donating to libraries, and the cost for two or three copies for yourself; otherwise, you could get stuck paying for a couple dozen books. After all, *you* did all the work; you should get something out of it. Most self-publishing companies will require the full payment up front.

Also check their publication time schedule. Christmas and the summer months are the busiest times since people want to have family histories ready as presents or available at the family reunion. Make sure you give yourself enough lead time if you need your book for a special occasion.

Commercial publishers will publish your book, absorbing all the costs of publication and marketing. In return, they make the profit; you receive royalties, usually 10 percent or less. The thing that your book must have in order for a commercial publisher to be interested in it is audience appeal. Most family histories have a limited readership and market: family members. This is why it is nearly impossible to find someone to publish it for you. But by adding historical context and writing it as a narrative—not just names and dates—you have automatically made your family history interesting to someone other than a relative. If you feel you are an accomplished writer and have successfully written a narrative account of your ancestors, placing them into historical perspective, you may be able to find a commercial publisher who will handle the costs, distribution, and marketing. Gay Talese did it. Ian Frazier did it. It's possible you could find someone to publish it, too, although it helps to have prior writing and publishing experience and an agent. It certainly cannot hurt to send a proposal to a publisher. Check the current *Writer's Market* (available in bookstores) for publishers who might be interested in your manuscript. For information on publishers, literary agents, and writing book proposals, see Jeff Herman's *Insider's Guide to Book Editors, Publishers, and Literary Agents.*

Marketing

Assuming you are going to self-publish, how do you know how many copies to have printed? Send out a prepublication notice to every relative and descendant you know of and to libraries that may want to purchase the book. So that non-genealogist relatives aren't confused between your legitimate family history and a bogus book offer that could arrive in their mailbox at the same time as yours, print your prepublication offer on your stationery letterhead. You may have even contacted most of these people for their family information if your book includes all descendants of an Italian couple. Here's a sample letter:

> Dear _____,
>
> After many years of research, I have completed the *Ebetino and Vallarelli Family History*. Thanks to everyone who contributed stories and information.
>
> The book will be available the beginning of August. It will be a hardcover volume, containing approximately 125 pages, including photographs, maps, and documents. The book is a narrative account of Salvatore and Angelina (Vallarelli) Ebetino and their lives in Italy and America. It also includes a genealogy of all their known descendants.
>
> Since there will be a limited number of copies printed, please return the enclosed order form by 28 April if you would like to reserve a copy. The cost is $—.— plus $2.50 postage.

After you know the number of copies that have been reserved, tack on at least another dozen copies. Once one relative shows your book to another, you may get additional orders. Also add to your print run the number of copies you think you will want to donate to libraries and to send to genealogical journals for review. For example, I donated copies of my book to the Family History Library in Salt Lake City; the Daughters of the American Revolution Library in Washington, DC; and the public library in Rye, New York, where the Ebetinos lived. In hindsight, I should also have donated copies to the Center for Migration Studies, the Italian American Heritage Center, the Immigration History Research Center, and the Ellis Island Research Library (see Appendix B).

I also sent two copies to the Library of Congress in order to obtain a copyright (discussed later) and one each to the *National Genealogical Society Quarterly* and *The New York Genealogical and Biographical Record* to be reviewed. After the reviews were published, I received orders from several libraries and a few individuals. Unfortunately, by then, I had run out of copies, so it's better to have a few too many than not enough.

Protecting Your Work

You've put a lot of work into your family history book. In order to protect your work, you should register it with the copyright office. Write to the Library of Congress, Register of Copyrights, Washington, DC 20002, to obtain information. You'll need to send two copies of your book along with a fee, about $20. Your book will also become part of the Library of Congress collection.

The Final Camera-Ready Copy

A guide I wish had been available when I did my book is Patricia Law Hatcher's *Producing a Quality Family History*. If the plan is to self-publish, then this is a wonderfully helpful book for formatting and designing the layout of your family history manuscript on your computer, as well as discussing all aspects of producing a book. I wouldn't do a self-published family history again without Hatcher's book.

Indexes

A family history is useless if it doesn't have an index. But to make your book even more valuable to people beyond the name-seekers, include subjects in your index. A subject index includes social history topics like fashion, food, work, childbirth, women, disease, place names, passenger ships' names, and ethnic groups. Many computer software packages have indexing features. Check your computer manuals to learn how to use them.

Time to Relax and Take a Trip to Italy

It's done. There is no greater thrill than when that box of books arrives at your doorstep from the publisher. The feeling you will have when you open the top copy, see your name on the cover and title page, and smell the newness of your book is unlike any other. Do you realize what you have accomplished? You have made your ancestors immortal. You cared enough about your heritage to document their lives for all eternity. Congratulations! Sit back, enjoy the feeling, and start planning a trip to Italy! I finally am doing just that.

To come of fine lineage is not a matter for personal pride or boastfullness, since we have had nothing to do with the value of our inheritance. But to live up to that lineage, to its traditions, its standards, its ideals; to hand it down to others, unlowered and unmarred—that is something for which we may well congratulate ourselves.

Author unknown

Appendix A
An Example of an Italian-American Family History Narrative

Excerpt taken from the forthcoming book
Italians in Transition: A Four Generation Perspective of the
Vallarelli Family
by Sharon DeBartolo Carmack

Southern Italian Peasant Life

There is no argument that our lives in the 1990s are dramatically different from our grandparents' generation. But for peasants like the Vallarelli family, who lived in southern Italy during the 1660s to 1920s, one generation's lifestyle was remarkably like the next and probably no different from the generations who came before.

The Vallarelli family had a long history of peasant life. Accessible birth, marriage, and death records from Terlizzi, Bari, Italy, document that Felice and Lucia (Ruta) Vallarelli, as of the 1830s, were *contadini* (peasant farmers) and remained so throughout their lifetimes.[1] These small landholders, who generally lived in villages like Terlizzi, rented land from absentee landlords. Most *contadini* had a one to three hour walk to the fields each morning and evening from

---

(NOTE: In the following footnotes, FHL refers to the Family History Library microfilm at Salt Lake City, Utah; and NARA refers to the National Archives Records Administration)

[1] By "accessible birth, marriage, and death records," I mean those records available on microfilm from the Family History Library in Salt Lake City, UT. For Terlizzi, the vital records span 1809 to 1865, although they are not inclusive for each event. For example, the birth records start with 1817; death records are available for 1809, then there is an eight-year gap with no available death records until 1817; marriage records begin with 1824. In the birth records for all of the children of Felice and Lucia (Ruta) Vallarelli, Felice is listed as a *contadino*, and Lucia as a *contadina*.

their homes. By 1806 most European peasants were emancipated from feudal control, but the peasantry in Italy was still bonded and offered the Vallarellis and other *contadini* few opportunities to rise socially or economically. Essentially, "the question for [rural Italian] peasants was not contentment but survival, not self-fulfillment but familial obligation, not advancement but stability."[2]

Surviving everyday life was a challenge in itself. Along with natural disasters such as earthquakes, droughts, and flooding, nineteenth-century peasant families also had to deal with frequent outbreaks of smallpox, meningitis, typhoid, cholera, and malaria.[3] Malnutrition was another problem for peasant families. They rarely ate meat; their diet consisted mainly of rice, fava beans, bread, pasta, and polenta (a type of corn meal mush). In the region of Apulia where the Vallarellis lived, *contadini* ate little but black barley bread. This type of diet—unbalanced, lacking in vitamins, high in complex carbohydrates, and low in protein—caused a common deficiency disease known as pellagra. Pellagra is a severe niacin deficiency found in diets where corn is a main part of the diet. Symptoms included scarlet lips and tongue, skin lesions, and abdominal discomfort and distention.[4]

With such diseases and malnutrition against them, many families lost several children, and parents were considered fortunate if they lived long enough to see any of their children marry and reproduce. Felice and Lucia were one of the fortunate couples who lost few of their children and lived to see at least three of their children marry and provide them with grandchildren.[5] Two of Felice and Lucia's children died in infancy; one child, Giuseppe, died in his twenties, having never married. Arcangela Raffaella, Lucia's fifth child, was born on the 17th of August in 1840 and died three days later.[6] Her death certificate did not reveal a cause of death, which was common. Felice and Lucia lost another infant, Pietro, who was

---

[2] Rudolph M. Bell, *Fate and Honor, Family and Village: Demographic and Cultural Change in Rural Italy since 1800* (Chicago: The University of Chicago Press, 1979), 1–7; quote from p. 7.

[3] Denis Mack Smith, *Italy: A Modern History* (Ann Arbor: The University of Michigan Press, 1959, 1969), 258; *The Merck Manual*, 13th ed. (Rahway, NJ: Merck Sharp and Dohme, 1977), 94–95.

[4] Mack Smith, *Italy*, pp. 40, 150; Bell, *Fate and Honor, Family and Village*, p. 137; *The Merck Manual*, 1162–63.

[5] The microfilmed death records for Terlizzi end with 1865. There are no records for Felice or Lucia, and they are still listed as living when Michele and Maria marry in 1858 and 1860, respectively.

[6] Birth record for Arcangela Raffaella Vallarelli, 1840, atto #378, Terlizzi, Italy, FHL #1640622; death record for Arcangela Raffaella Vallarelli, 1840, atto #313, p. 157, Terlizzi, Italy, FHL #1640608.

born nine years after Arcangela. He was forty days old when he died in March 1849.[7]

While death may have been a frequent aspect of the peasant family's life, it was never taken lightly. The death of a child caused parents extreme grief. The custom of naming children after grandparents and the use of necronyms—naming the next-born child with the same name as a deceased child who carried a grandparent's name—further demonstrated the importance of procreation and perpetuation of *la famiglia*.[8] In the Vallarelli family, after Arcangela Raffaella died, a boy was born next and was christened in the masculine form of the name: Arcangelo Raffaello. This was Lucia's mother's name.[9]

As Felice and Lucia's children were marrying and beginning families of their own, Italy was undergoing political changes that ultimately had an effect on the next generations' decision to emigrate. Before 1860, Italy was divided into eight separate states, with all but one ruled by foreign governments or the papacy. The movement known as *Risorgimento* was to unite Italy and remove foreign rule.[10] While the movement reached success and the north and central part of Italy prospered, the south—the *Mezzogiorno*—remained unaffected, and the peasant class continued to sink further into poverty. Starting a decade after unification, peasants began to leave the country in substantial numbers:

1876 100,000 left per year
1901 half-million left annually
1914 5–6 million Italians were living abroad while 35 million remained
1927 9 million Italians were living abroad[11]

Felice and Lucia's son Fortunato, who married Isabella Veneto in 1870,[12] watched all seven of his children leave Italy and start life anew in America. One by one, starting in 1906, a son, then a daughter, then another son, bid their parents and homeland good-bye, until they were all pulled by the opportunity of a better life in America.

---

[7] Death record for Pietro Vallarelli, 1849, atto #111, Terlizzi, Italy, FHL #1640609.

[8] Bell, *Fate and Honor, Family and Village*, 44–45; quote from p. 44.

[9] Birth record for Arcangelo Raffaelle Vallarelli, 1842, atto #52, Terlizzi, Italy, FHL #1640622; Lucia's parents' names are listed on her children's birth records.

[10] Jerre Mangione and Ben Morreale, *La Storia: Five Centuries of the Italian American Experience* (New York: HarperCollins, 1992), 31.

[11] Mack Smith, *Italy*, 239–40.

[12] Marriage abstract of Fortunato Vallarelli and Isabella Veneto, 1870, Atto #73; abstract obtained from Frank DeBartolo on a trip to Terlizzi, Italy.

The Immigrant Experience: From Steerage to Ellis Island

For many southern Italian peasants like the children of Fortunato and Isabella Vallarelli, the decision to leave Italy and head for a new country across the Atlantic was the result of several factors, many of them economic. In the old country, *contadini* earned about 20 cents a day; in America, they could earn $1 a day as laborers.[13]

The peak years of immigration to America were between 1901 and 1914, and this is the time span when the adult children of Fortunato and Isabella emigrated from Italy. These Vallarelli siblings followed the common pattern of chain migration, where the first arrivals paid for their relatives' passage and provided temporary lodging when newcomers arrived. Felice was the first to leave in 1906, followed by his sisters Angelina and Maria in 1910, sister Lucia and brother Frank in 1913, sister Antonia in 1914, and, finally, brother Michelle by 1919. Though the immigrating Vallarellis traveled in different years, on different ships, with some arriving at different ports, they all left from the Port of Naples and traveled in third class or steerage. Their travel experiences can be reconstructed based on the typical experiences of other immigrants during this mass exodus.[14]

A one-way steerage ticket cost about $35 at the turn of the twentieth century. This was the equivalent of several months—if not years—of savings for many *contadini* like the Vallarellis. After acquiring identity papers and a passport, emigrants traveled to the port city and stayed in a tiny, mock village set up by the steamship company. Here, they were quarantined for five days in a "pest house" and given antiseptic baths. The men were given short haircuts, and both men and women had their scalps washed with a soft soap, carbolic acid (a disinfectant), and petroleum. Since the steamship com-

---

[13] Edward Oxford, "Hope, Tears, and Remembrance," *American History Illustrated* (Oct 1990): 36.

[14] Passenger arrival lists for the Vallarelli siblings: Felice Vallarelli, *Italia*, leaving from Naples, 25 Apr 1906, arriving at New York, 10 May 1906, group 7, list 137, line 23, NARA Microcopy T715, roll 706, vol. 1564. Angelina and Maria Vallarelli, *Verona*, leaving from Naples, 5 Feb 1910, arriving at New York, 18 Feb 1910, NARA Microcopy T715, roll 1413, vol. 3109. Lucia Vallarelli, *Canopic*, sailing from Naples on 15 Jan 1913, arriving at Boston, 29 Jan 1913, list 7, lines 3–8, NARA Microcopy T843, roll 190, vol. 323. Francesco Vallarelli, *Stampalia*, leaving Naples 23 July 1913, arriving New York, 5 Aug 1913, list 4, line 20, NARA Microcopy T715, roll 2146, vol. 4866. Antonia Vallarelli, *Sant' Ana*, sailing from Naples on 29 May 1914, arriving New York, 12 June 1914, group 5, line 28, NARA T715, roll 2333, vol. 5344. No passenger arrival list has been found for Michelle Vallarelli; his date of immigration is estimated based on his marriage in America. Thomas M. Pitkin, *Keepers of the Gate: A History of Ellis Island* (New York: New York University Press, 1975), 67.

panies had to absorb the cost of return passage for anyone who did not pass the health inspections in America, the emigrants were given medical examinations and vaccinations before departure.[15]

Buon Viaggio

After a stay at the pest house for at least five days, the waiting Italians were then taken through the streets to the docks. Steamship representatives compiled the ship's manifest, or list of passengers. They recorded such information as name, age, sex, occupation, and marital status; last residence; final destination in the United States; if ever in the United States before, when, where, and for how long; if going to join a relative, the relative's name, address, and relationship; whether able to read and write; whether in possession of a train ticket to the final destination; who paid the passage; amount of money the passenger was carrying; whether the passenger had ever been in prison, almshouse, or institution for the insane, or was a polygamist; the passenger's state of health; a personal description that included height, complexion, color of hair and eyes, identifying marks; place of birth; and name and address of closest living relative in native country.[16]

Most steamships were capable of carrying about 1,500 third-class passengers, but many vessels were overcrowded in steerage, transporting several hundred more than capacity. On Felice Vallarelli's ship, *Italia*, the maximum capacity in steerage was exceeded by about 340 people. Steerage was so named because the third-class compartment was located below deck near the steering mechanism. There was little ventilation in this area. The floors were wooden and sprinkled with sand. Although they were swept daily, they were not washed during an entire two-week voyage.[17]

The large steerage compartment contained tiers of bunks; each iron berth had a straw mattress covered with a slip of white canvas.

---

[15] Oxford, 36; Thomas Dunne and Wilton Tifft, *Ellis Island* (New York: W.W. Norton & Co., 1971), no page numbers; Mary J. Shapiro, *Gateway to Liberty: The Story of the Statue of Liberty and Ellis Island* (New York: Vintage Books, 1986), 77, 85–87; Willard Price, "What I Learned by Traveling from Naples to New York in the Steerage," *The Italians: Social Backgrounds of an American Group*, edited by Eugene Bucchioni and Francesco Cordasco (Clifton, NJ: Augustus M. Kelley Publ., 1974; article originally published in *World Outlook* 3 [Oct 1917]: 3–5, 14), 104.

[16] Shapiro, 78. The content of passenger arrival lists varied depending on the year of immigration. See John Philip Colletta, *They Came in Ships* (Salt Lake City: Ancestry Publishing, 1989), 27–35.

[17] Shapiro, 78.

There was no pillow; in its place was each passenger's life preserver. A short, light-weight blanket was also provided and became part of the emigrant's possessions. To the travelers, the berth became their space, serving as bed, clothes and towel rack, and baggage storage area.[18]

No real provisions were made for them to be clean. On most ships, there were no hooks for clothes, no trash containers, and no cans for seasickness. It is not surprising that emigrants had a reputation for being filthy; they simply had no choice.[19]

Each passenger was supplied with eating utensils, usually a fork, spoon, and tin lunch pail. A typical breakfast might consist of coffee and a biscuit. For lunch, soup and one dish with meat every five days. For supper, they would be fed a dish with meat, wine, and bread. After meals, the passengers washed their own dishes, using their own soap and towels that they brought on board with them. Sometimes there might only be one faucet of warm water. With nearly 2,000 people waiting to use it, some may have opted to get the grease off their tins with cold, salt water.[20]

On many steamships, there were only two washrooms, and these were used by both men and women at the same time. The washrooms contained small basins that the passengers used to wash their greasy tins, as a laundry tub for their clothing, and as a receptacle to bathe their bodies. There was no special cleaning of these basins in between uses, and these were the only containers to be found for seasickness.[21]

The passengers were supposed to undergo daily medical examinations during the voyage; however, they usually received only two—one at the beginning of the voyage and one toward the end. Lined up in a single file, a ship's doctor casually glanced over the travelers while an assistant would punch six holes at a time in a health inspection card. One punch was to represent each of the daily exams. Toward the end of the voyage, this "examination" process was repeated, making it look like the passengers had received an exam every day.[22]

---

[18] Edith Abbott, *Immigration: Select Documents and Case Records* (Chicago: University of Chicago Press, 1924), 82–86.

[19] Abbott, 82–86.

[20] Abbott, 82–86.

[21] Abbott, 82–86.

[22] Abbott, 82–86.

As one passenger recalled:

> [We lived for two weeks] in a disorder and in surroundings that offended every sense. Only the fresh breeze from the sea overcame the sickening odors. The vile language of the men, the screams of the women defending themselves, the crying of the children . . . practically every sound that reached the ear irritated beyond endurance. . . . Everything was dirty, sticky, and disagreeable to the touch. . . . Worse than this was the general air of immorality. . . . All around [there was] improper, indecent, and forced mingling of men and women who were total strangers and often did not understand one word of the same language.[23]

On rough voyages the decks would reek of vomit. Since they could not use the small open deck allotted to them during this time, the immigrants spent day and night in their berths, with the steerage hatches shut tight, "listening to the sick moan and groan." Besides the stench of unwashed bodies and vomit, travelers endured vermin such as rats, roaches, and lice. For those who did not survive the voyage, a burial at sea was common. One can only imagine the heartache of having to watch as a loved one, wrapped in a canvas shroud, was thrown overboard.[24]

Is it no wonder, then, that these people would "arrive at the journey's end with a mind unfit for healthy, wholesome impressions and with a body weakened and unfit for the hardships that were involved in the beginning of life in the new land?"[25]

When the weather was nice, however, the immigrants could wander along their allotted deck. Though the first and second class passengers were provided with entertainment, the third class had to provide their own. Singing and dancing was a common divergence to the otherwise daily monotony of steamship travel in the early twentieth century.[26]

After two weeks of these poor conditions, ships headed for the Port of New York passed through a narrow waterway between

---

[23] Abbott, 82–86.

[24] Quote from an interview with Fred Ebetino, 1990; Alexander DeConde, *Half Bitter, Half Sweet: An Excursion into Italian-American History* (New York: Charles Scribner's Sons, 1971), 71; Edward Marshall, "Makes Six Ocean Trips to Study Steerage and Reform. Ernest C. Cotterill reports on the bad state of affairs among the immigrants on some ships and offers recommendations for improvement of conditions," *New York Times*, Sunday, 30 Nov 1913, part VI, p. 10; Oxford, 40.

[25] August C. Bolino, *The Ellis Island Source Book* (Washington, DC: Kensington Historical Press, 1985), 13.

[26] Marshall, 10.

Brooklyn and Staten Island. Getting their first glimpse of America, the newcomers focused on the Statue of Liberty that was unveiled in New York Harbor on October 25, 1886. Every passenger's face was no doubt "lit up with hope and fear, joy and sorrow. Hope for success in the new land; . . . fear of the unknown future; joy that the long-dreaded voyage is over; and sorrow at the memories tugging" at their hearts. Passengers destined for other United States ports, like Lucia (Vallarelli) DeBartolo and her children who landed at the Port of Boston in 1913, missed this symbolic greeting upon their arrival to America.[27]

A small cutter approached the incoming ship, where a United States doctor boarded and checked everyone for obvious signs of illness. He also checked with the ship's doctor for any contagious diseases. If there were none, the ship came to port at a wharf. This was where the first and second class passengers were docked. The third class, however, was loaded onto barges and taken to Ellis Island.[28]

Like the steamship, the barge was overcrowded, cramming 900 people onto one built for 600. This might have been acceptable for the short trip down the river, but each barge usually had to wait hours to disembark its passengers—and it contained few toilet facilities.[29]

While the newcomers waited to dock, they gazed at a huge, brick, castle-like building. The main building on Ellis Island was opened on December 17, 1900, after a fire had destroyed the original wooden building in 1897.[30]

The first structure, made of Georgia pine, was constructed for the opening of Ellis Island on New Year's Day, 1892. Two years earlier, this site had been chosen as an immigrant receiving station to re-place Castle Garden on the southern tip of Manhattan, which had been in operation since 1855. Ellis Island was a small island where the water was too shallow for ships to dock. Over the following years after the island reopened in 1900, it was more than doubled in size with landfill.[31]

---

[27] Bolino, 14–15; quote from Oxford, 42; passenger arrival manifest listing Lucia Vallarelli, *Canopic*.

[28] Bolino, 14–15; Shapiro, 121. Other ports also had immigrant receiving stations.

[29] Shapiro, 155.

[30] Shapiro, 130–31, 138.

[31] Shapiro, 106, 115–19.

Processing at Ellis Island

As the immigrants landed from the barge, they were tagged with a number that corresponded to their number (placement) on the ship's passenger list. As a group they were led into the main building where their baggage was inspected. They were then led up a stairway where, unbeknownst to them, the first of a series of medical inspections took place. Inspectors were stationed at various points along the stairway and watched for obvious signs of defects, derangements, and heart and lung problems. Noted immigrants were stopped and had their dark clothing marked on the front shoulder with chalk, such as with the letter "H," indicating heart problems.[32]

At the first station in the huge Registry Hall, a surgeon checked each arrival's health inspection card from aboard ship. After stamping it, he handed it back to the immigrant and watched. The unsuspecting person would look to see what the inspector had stamped on the card and inadvertently revealed any eye problems.[33]

Even before many emigrants had left Italy, they were warned by earlier travelers about the second station's exam: "Beware of the eye man." He was checking for trachoma, a highly contagious eye disease that caused blindness. Anyone found to have it was immediately deported.[34]

"To turn the eyelid, I used the good old buttoner," stated Dr. Grover Kempf, a U.S. public health physician at Ellis Island. "This was a little loop [used] to button shoes; [we] used [it] to turn the eyelid. It was the most efficient way of turning the eyes ever devised."[35]

As one might imagine, this exam was greatly feared and most painful. But every immigrant experienced it—both young and old— the Vallarellis included.[36]

Further problems discovered during these exams were again indicated on the immigrant's clothing in chalk: "C" for conjunctivitis, "Ct" for trachoma, "Ft" feet problems, "Pg" pregnant, "K" hernia, and "X" for possible mental retardation. These marked persons were taken out of line and given more thorough examinations.[37]

---

[32] Bolino, 14–15; Shapiro, 160; Pitkin, 68–69.

[33] Bolino, 14–15; Pitkin, 68–69.

[34] Shapiro, 159–60; quote from Oxford, 42.

[35] Fred Wasserman, ed., *Ellis Island: An Illustrated History of the Immigrant Experience* (New York: Macmillan Publ. Co., 1991), 114.

[36] Shapiro, 159–60.

[37] Shapiro, 160.

After completing the medical exams, the newcomers were instructed to sit in a waiting pen; each manifest group having its own area. While they waited, they heard the sounds of mingling languages, children crying, and guards yelling.[38]

A registry clerk called up one group at a time. These clerks, dressed in military-style uniforms, frightened many of the immigrants. Some had left Italy to avoid military conscription. Now the first person they had to deal with reeked of this type of authority.[39]

With hundreds of interpreters to help, the clerk, "armed with a copy of the manifest sheet," would ask the immigrants the same questions and compare the answers. If there were any discrepancies, he could have the new arrival detained. Two of the most troublesome questions for Italians were "Do you have a job waiting?" and "Who paid for your passage?" In 1885, the United States government had outlawed labor contracts. One of the most common ways for Italians to pay their passage was to have an "indenture" with a *padrone*. A *padrone* recruited workers in Italy, offering to pay the *contadini's* passage. The emigrant would repay his passage once in America, with interest, by working off his debt. On the other hand, if there was no job waiting, then the immigrant had to convince the clerk that he was not likely to become a public charge.[40]

The arrivals were never told the results of any of the exams. They were simply whisked onto another waiting area until their names were called so they might leave the island.[41]

Women's Immigration Experiences

Women had a slightly different immigration experience from men. Many of the women who arrived during the peak years came alone or with small children. Typically, most of the women who immigrated were young, healthy, and may have only been married a few months or perhaps a couple of years before their husbands embarked for America. Their husbands had come to America first, working to save enough money to pay for their wives' and children's passage. Once the passage money arrived, each woman had the responsibility of selling furniture and possessions that could not be carried

---

[38] Shapiro, 165, Bolino, 17.

[39] Shapiro, 165; Wasserman, 119.

[40] First quote, Pitkin, 22–23; quoted questions, Joseph Giordano, ed. *The Italian American Catalog* (New York, Doubleday, 1986), 203; Thomas A. Bass, "A New Life Begins for Island of Hope and Tears," *Smithsonian* (June 1990): 90.

[41] Oxford, 68–70.

aboard ship. She had to obtain the necessary traveling documents and steamship tickets, then find a way to get to the port city. Most women had never even gone beyond the borders of their native villages. Most certainly, they had never experienced dealing with bureaucrats. Some women—married and single—were forced to submit to a demand for sexual favors before they were given the papers they needed to emigrate.[42]

Unescorted women, like Antonia Vallarelli who arrived in 1914, were detained at Ellis Island until someone arrived to pick them up. Antonia was held until her sister, Maria Riccio, claimed her the afternoon of Antonia's arrival. The United States government did not want to encourage prostitution or white slave trading. When a single man, claiming to be the fiancé of a single woman, came to take her off the island, the wedding might take place on Ellis Island before she was allowed to leave with him. This was one way to ensure that the man was really her husband-to-be.[43]

Even some women traveling with children were held until someone came to claim them. Though Angelina (Vallarelli) Ebetino arrived in 1910 accompanied by her three small children, her eighteen-year-old unmarried sister, Maria, and a thirty-seven-year-old male cousin, Nicolo Callo, they were all detained overnight until Angelina's husband arrived at Ellis Island.[44]

Inspectors were also told to detain idiots, imbeciles, epileptics, the feeble minded, the senile, or the insane. Characteristics they watched for included talkativeness, smart aleckiness, eroticism or flirtyness, boisterousness, surliness, intoxication, confusion and disorientation, aimlessness, stuttering, and excessive friendliness.[45]

For those who were detained, there was nothing to do except sit on hard wooden benches and wait. The men and women were generally kept separated, but occasional visits to the roof garden allowed mingling and a time for children to run around a small playground. Representatives from immigrant-aid and patriotic societies such as the Society for the Protection of Italian Immigrants, the Daughters of the American Revolution, and the YMCA helped occupy the immigrants, teaching them English and how to be "good" Americans.[46]

---

[42] Mangione and Morreale, 92–94.

[43] Passenger arrival manifest listing Antonia Vallarelli, *Sant' Ana*; Bolino, 18, 20.

[44] Passenger arrival manifest listing Angelina Vallarelli, *Verona*.

[45] Bolino, 3.

[46] Shapiro, 153, 217–18; Gino C. Speranza, "How it Feels to be a Problem," *The Italians: Social Backgrounds of an American Ethnic Group*, edited by Eugene Bucchioni and Francesco Cordasco (Clifton, NJ: Augustus M. Kelley Publ., 1974, article originally published in *Charities* 12 [1904]: 457–463), 290.

For a time, there were separate dining halls for men and women, where detainees were sometimes fed without forks, spoons, or knives. If there happened to be an insufficient number of bowls or plates, they were likely to be reused, without washing, until all had been fed.[47]

A typical 1906 menu at Ellis Island was as follows:

Breakfast

coffee with milk and sugar

bread and butter, plus crackers and milk for women and children

Lunch

beef stew, boiled potatoes, and rye bread

plus crackers and milk for women and children

Supper

baked beans, stewed prunes, and rye bread

tea with milk and sugar, plus crackers and milk for women and children

One delicacy served on the island was prune sandwiches. Ellis Island ordered twenty million prunes a year. By 1905, they were served only twice weekly. This was not because the treat was becoming monotonous, but because, as one waiter described it, the floor was like a skating rink from all the discarded, slimy prune pits. In the dining rooms, many Italians ate their first banana—peel and all.[48]

The Possibility of Being Rejected

As early as 1893, the Supreme Court had ruled that incoming migrants did not have a right to land and had no right to a legal hearing if there was a decision to deport them. If held for the Board of Special Inquiry on Ellis Island, newcomers were not allowed to confer with relatives or an attorney unless they were given an unfavorable decision to be deported.[49]

------

[47] Shapiro, 142–43.

[48] Wasserman, 154; Shapiro, 144; Alice Hall, "New Life for Ellis Island," *National Geographic* (Sept 1990): 95.

[49] Bolino, 21, 25.

About 1,000 people each month were considered "undesirable." This was why the immigrants referred to the receiving station as the Island of Hope and Tears. Being diseased or likely to be a public charge was cause for immediate deportation. By 1909, if an immigrant did not have at least $25 cash in his possession upon arrival, he was deported.[50]

Returning to the homeland meant disgrace. All hopes and dreams were gone. These immigrants had sold all their possessions to pay for their passage. Agonizing decisions had to be made when one member of the family was not admitted. The question became do they say good-bye to their family member, or do they all return to Italy together?[51]

Henry Curran, a commissioner of Ellis Island, wrote this about the deportees in 1923:

> Day by day the barges took them from Ellis Island back to the ships again, back to the ocean, back to—what? As they trooped aboard the big barges under my window, carrying their heavy bundles, some in their colorful native costumes worn to celebrate their first glad day in free America, some carrying little American flags, most of them quietly weeping, they twisted something in my heart.[52]

A morgue and crematory were installed on Ellis Island, and several immigrants committed suicide during its history. Others took their lives by jumping overboard on the voyage back.[53]

Those who passed the inspections also had to deal with bribery, cheating, and petty thievery by other immigrants and by Ellis Island personnel. Though each new commissioner planned to clean up these matters, the conditions continued to exist as long as the processing center remained active.[54]

Admittance into America

Once the immigrants' names were read, telling them that they were allowed to leave, they were then taken to the money exchange office to trade their foreign currency. After that, they were escorted to the ferries that would take them to other transportation, leading to their final destinations.[55]

---

[50] Shapiro, 199; Oxford, 69.

[51] Shapiro, 210.

[52] Oxford, 69.

[53] Dunne, no page numbers.

[54] Shapiro, 138–39.

[55] "Island of Hope—Island of Tears," video cassette (New York: Ellis Island Immigration Museum Film, 1992).

All of the Vallarelli siblings passed through Ellis Island without incident. The next hurdle for each of them was living in America. "Everything, human contact, work, language, living quarters, climate, and food becomes a problem to be resolved, a difficulty to overcome. They suddenly realize that they know nothing anymore."[56] They must begin again.

Was it all really worth it? For the Vallarelli siblings and thousands of other Italian immigrants the hurdles they had to overcome were worth starting their life all over again in America. It gave them, their children, and their children's children opportunities none of them would have had if they had stayed in southern Italy. Had they stayed in the Old Country, their lives would have remained unchanged. Even into the twentieth century, they would have exposed their families to famines, malnutrition, droughts, diseases, and natural disasters. While their roots extended for several generations in Terlizzi, a better outcome awaited them in America. Passing through the Golden Door at Ellis Island was the Vallarellis' golden opportunity.

Give me your tired, your poor,
Your huddled masses yearning to breathe free,
The wretched refuse of your teeming shore,
Send these, the homeless, the tempest-tost, to me,
I lift my lamp beside the golden door!

—Emma Lazarus, *The New Colossus*

---

[56] Quote from Francesco P. Cerase, "Expectations and Reality: A Case Study of Return Migration from the United States to Southern Italy," *International Migration Review* 8 (1974): 24.

Appendix B
Ethnic Collections and Archives in the United States

ITALIAN AMERICAN HERITAGE CENTER
Catholic University
620 Michigan Avenue, N.E.
Washington, DC 20064

The Italian American Heritage Center is a non-profit organization located at Catholic University in Washington, DC. The Center promotes "interest in the history and culture of the Italian people, the experiences and contributions of Italian immigrants to the United States, and the continuing relationships between the peoples and nations of the United States and Italy." In meeting its goal, the Center hosts numerous academic and cultural programs. The Center also maintains a library/archives, a museum, and seminar rooms. Included in the Heritage Center Archives will be an Italian American Immigration Data Bank to aid in tracing family histories. Data will be gathered in connection with the Ellis Island Restoration projects, and Italian Americans are invited to send their family information to be included in this data bank. Manuscript collections, correspondence, reports, notes, clippings, pamphlets, and photographs pertaining to Italian Americans will make up the archival collection.

IMMIGRATION HISTORY RESEARCH CENTER
University of Minnesota
826 Berry Street
St. Paul, MN 55114

The Immigration History Research Center, located at the University of Minnesota in St. Paul, has a collection that focuses "primarily on the experiences of immigrants and generally consists of documentation they themselves generated as opposed to information recorded by government officials or others involved in processing newcomers through American ports or assigning citizenship." Items found at the IHRC include ethnic newspapers and serials; fraternal society materials; church records and publications; manuscript collections; oral histories, memoirs, and family histories; and a reference collection. According to *The Immigration History Research Cen-*

ter: A Guide to Collections, "the Italian American collection is one of the IHRC's largest, with ca. 1,400 items." More than 400 different Italian and Italian-American newspapers and serials are available, with many on microfilm. Another large portion of this collection is the records of the Order Sons of Italy in America, about which a separate guide has been published. Advance notice of research visits is encouraged. The non-microfilmed collection does not circulate, but many items are available on microfilm through interlibrary loan.

ELLIS ISLAND RESEARCH LIBRARY
Liberty Island/Ellis Island
New York, NY 10004

Ellis Island, the major immigrant receiving center in the United States between 1891 and 1957, has undergone restoration of its main building and is now one of New York's largest museums. It also contains a research library and oral history collection. Among its collections are photographs and periodicals pertaining to the history of the island. More than 700 interviews have been collected under the oral history project. Paul E. Sigrist, oral historian for the project, has compiled "The Complete Ellis Island Oral History Project Interview List." This is an unpublished manuscript available at the Ellis Island Research Library and at the Family History Library in Salt Lake City. The interview must have been conducted by Ellis Island employees to be included in this collection. Interviews by reporters, independent historians, or others are not maintained in the island's collection.

The Ellis Island Foundation is in the process of seeking funds to construct "The American Family Immigration History Center." In the first phase, data from ships' manifests of passengers arriving at the Port of New York and Ellis Island, 1892–1924, will be entered into a computer database and made available to the public. In another phase, contributors will be able to add their immigrant ancestor's story into the database and include names of descendants and photographs. If you would like more information on this project or want to make a monetary contribution, write to the Statue of Liberty-Ellis Island Foundation, Inc., P.O. Box 1955, New York, NY 10117-1955.

Until this project is complete, however, passenger lists for the Port of New York will continue to be maintained at such repositories as the National Archives in Washington, DC, National Archives—Northeast Region, the New York Public Library, and the Family History Library in Salt Lake City. Ellis Island Board of Special Inquiry records may be found at the Immigration and Naturalization Service New York district office located at 26 Federal Plaza, Room 14-102, New York, NY 10278.

CENTER FOR MIGRATION STUDIES
209 Flagg Place
Staten Island, NY 10304-1148

The Center for Migration Studies is an educational, non-profit institute founded in 1964 to encourage the study of sociological, demographic, historical, economic, political, legislative, and pastoral aspects of human migration and ethnic group relations. It publishes the *International Migration Review*, a quarterly journal devoted to immigration and ethnicity; and *Migration Today*, a bimonthly magazine on migrants that discusses books, monographs, bibliographies, documents, and occasional papers. CMS also publishes from five to seven texts annually from conference proceedings, oral histories and monographs, to bibliographies and organization directories. Write to CMS for a listing of publications. The CMS library has more than 1,100 volumes in the field of migration and ethnicity. The archival holdings pertain primarily to the Italian-American experience and the role of the Catholic Church. A three-volume *Guide to the Archives* outlines the holdings.

BALCH INSTITUTE FOR ETHNIC STUDIES
18 South Seventh Street
Philadelphia, PA 19106

The Balch Institute is a six-story library/museum with the mission of documenting and interpreting American ethnic and immigration history. Its purpose is "to collect and preserve publications, archival and manuscript materials, photographs, and other sources that provide information on how and why immigrants came to North America and how they and their descendants adapted and lived after they arrived here." The library also consists of "more than 1,200 volumes, 40 manuscript collections, and 60 collections of historical photographs, plus dozens of periodical titles and other materials documenting the Italian-American experience." The primary focus of the collection, however, is on Italians in the Delaware Valley. A paper titled "Italian-American Resources at the Balch Institute Library," by R. Joseph Anderson, is available upon request. For further information on the collection, contact the reference librarian. The holdings are catalogued on the international OCLC (On-line Computer Library Center) database, and there is a published guide to the manuscript collections.

ITALIAN AMERICAN COLLECTION OF WESTERN PENNSYLVANIA
4338 Bigelow Boulevard
Pittsburgh, PA 15213

Part of the Historical Society of Western Pennsylvania's Pittsburgh Regional Ethnic Archives and Museum Collection, this new acquistion on Italian Americans is to maintain and provide access to materials relating to the history of Western Pennsylvania's Italian-American communities. The historical society gathers the materials of organizations, churches, businesses, individuals and families, and social and professional groups.

ITALIAN AMERICAN COLLECTION
San Francisco Public Library
Civic Center
San Francisco, CA 94102

Focusing on the mass influx of Italians to northern California in the late nineteenth century and early twentieth century, the Italian American Collection is housed in the San Francisco Room of the main library. The holdings also include materials concerning Italians in the West.

Other Collections
Other repositories with collections on Italian Americans are the New York Public Library, Fifth Avenue at 42nd Street, New York, NY 10018; New Haven Public Library, 133 Elm Street, New Haven, CT 06510; and Providence Public Library, 150 Empire Street, Providence, RI 02903. Also, university libraries such as those at Yale, Columbia, Harvard, and others located where Italians tended to settle will have collections on the Italian immigrant experience. Local historical society collections should also be checked.

Appendix C
Italian-American Organizations

Note: The reader should write for current membership fees.

American Italian Heritage Association
P.O. Box 419
Morrisville, NY 13408

Records and preserves Italian heritage and culture. Holds annual spring and fall conferences. Supports a museum dedicated to the memory of Italian immigrants who came to America. Publishes a bimonthly newsletter.

American Italian Historical Association
209 Flagg Place
Staten Island, NY 10304

An interdisciplinary association to promote understanding of the Italian experience in America. Publishes a quarterly newsletter and the proceedings of annual conferences.

The Italian Genealogical Society of America, Inc.
P.O. Box 8571
Cranston, RI 02920-8571

Promotes Italian-American research in the field of Italian genealogy (research, writing, lecturing, and instruction). Publishes a quarterly newsletter and sponsors lectures, workshops, and seminars.

National Italian American Foundation
666 11th St., N.W., Suite 800
Washington, DC 20077-0380

Dedicated to preserving Italian heritage and values by integrating and retaining them in the mainstream of American life. Publishes a bimonthly newsletter and the *Ambassador* quarterly magazine.

Italian Genealogical Group
7 Grayon Drive
Dix Hills, NY 11746

Promotes and encourages the study of Italian family history. Offers workshops, seminars, and a newsletter.

Pursuing Our Italian Names Together
P.O. Box 2977
Palos Verdes, CA 90274

Network of those interested in Italian genealogy. Publishes a quarterly magazine, *POINTers*. Maintains a database of Italian surnames and people researching them.

Bibliography

Research Guides and Record Abstracts

Andreozzi, John. *Guide to the Records of the Order Sons of Italy in America*. St. Paul: Immigration History Research Center, 1989.

Bentley, Elizabeth Petty. *The Genealogist's Address Book*. 3d ed. Baltimore: Genealogical Publishing Co., 1995.

Bourque, Monique and R. Joseph Anderson. *A Guide to Manuscript and Microfilm Collections of the Research Library of the Balch Institute for Ethnic Studies*. Philadelphia: Balch Institute, 1992.

Brigham, Clarence S. *History and Bibliography of American Newspapers, 1690–1820*. 2 vols. Worcester, MA: American Antiquarian Society, 1947.

Carmack, Sharon DeBartolo. "Researching Italian-American Ancestry." *Reunions* (Autumn 1994): 30–31.

_____. "Ordering Records from the Immigration and Naturalization Service." *Reunions* (Summer 1994): 12.

Cole, Trafford R. *Italian Genealogical Records: How to Use Italian Civil, Ecclesiastical, and Other Records in Family History Research*. Salt Lake City: Ancestry Publishing, 1995.

Colletta, John P. *Finding Italian Roots: The Complete Guide for Americans*. Baltimore: Genealogical Publishing Co., 1993.

_____. *They Came in Ships*. 2d ed. rev. Salt Lake City: Ancestry Publishing, 1993.

DeAngelis, Priscilla Grindle. *Italian-American Genealogy: A Source Book*. Rockville, MD: Noteworthy Enterprises Publishing, 1994.

DiNinni, Ronald V. and Mary I. DiNinni. *Legacy of Life: Una Storia della Famiglia Italiana* [Lineages of families from Palmoli, Abruzzi, Italy]. 2 vols. Baltimore: Gateway Press, 1996.

Gale Directory of Publications and Broadcast Media. Detroit: Gale Research Co., annual.

Galli, Jonathan D. "Tips for Tracing Your Italian Ancestry." *NEHGS NEXUS* 13 (1996): 108–9.

Glazier, Ira A. and P. William Filby, eds. *Italians to America: Lists of Passengers Arriving at U.S. Ports 1880–1899*. 10 vols. Wilmington, DE: Scholarly Resources, 1993—.

Gregory, Winifred, ed. *American Newspapers, 1821–1936*. New York: H.W. Wilson Co., 1937.

Guide to Genealogical Research in the National Archives. Washington, DC: National Archives Trust Fund Board, rev. ed. 1985.

Humling, Virginia. *U.S. Catholic Sources: A Diocesan Research Guide*. Salt Lake City: Ancestry Publishing, 1996.

Immigrant and Passenger Arrivals: A Select Catalog of National Archives Microfilm Publications. Washington, DC: National Archives Trust Fund Board, rev. ed. 1991.

Library of Congress. *Newspapers in Microform: United States*. Washington, DC: Library of Congress, Catalog Publications Divisions, 1948 and supplements.

_____. *Newspapers in Microform: Foreign Countries*. Washington, DC: Library of Congress, Catalog Publications Divisions, 1948 and supplements.

Military Service Records: A Select Catalog of National Archives Microfilm Publications. Washington, DC: National Archives Trust Fund Board, 1985.

Moody, Suzanna and Joel Wurl. *The Immigration History Research Center: A Guide to Collections*. New York: Greenwood Press, 1991.

Morton Allan Directory of European Passenger Steamship Arrivals for the Years 1890 to 1930 at the Port of New York and for the Years 1904 to 1926 at the Ports of New York, Philadelphia, Boston, and Baltimore. Reprint. Baltimore: Genealogical Publishing Co., 1980.

Neagles, James C. *U.S. Military Records*. Salt Lake City: Ancestry Publishing, 1994.

Newman, John J. *American Naturalization Processes and Procedures, 1790–1985*. Indianapolis: Indiana Historical Society, 1985.

Robichaux, Albert J. *Italian-American Roots, Vol. 1 (1851–1861): Civil Records of Births-Marriages-Deaths of Alia, Sicily*. Rayne, LA: Hebert Publications, 1994.

Schaefer, Christina K. *The Center: A Guide to Genealogical Research in the National Capital Area*. Baltimore: Genealogical Publishing Co., 1996.

_____. *Naturalization Records of the United States*. Baltimore: Genealogical Publishing Co., 1997.

Sigrist, Paul E. "The Complete Ellis Island Oral History Project Interview List." Unpublished manuscript. Washington, DC: U.S. Department of the Interior, National Parks Service, n.d.

Tepper, Michael. *American Passenger Arrival Records: A Guide to the Records of Immigrants Arriving at American Ports by Sail and Steam.* Baltimore: Genealogical Publishing Co., 1993.

Lecture Audio Tapes
Tapes may be purchased through Repeat Performance, 2911 Crabapple Lane, Hobart, IN 46342.

Bockstruck, Lloyd. "Passenger and Immigration Records." DRC-28.

Carmack, Sharon DeBartolo. "Building Character: Writing Your Ancestor's Story." SD-186.

_____. "Italian-American Character: Understanding Your Ancestors for Better Research Success." RNY-101.

_____. "Flesh on the Bones: Placing Your Ancestors into Historical Context." JF-176.

_____. "The Immigrant Experience: From Steerage to Ellis Island." RNY-114.

Colletta, John Philip. "Coming to America: Research Your Ancestor's Immigration Stories." JF-22.

_____. "Immigration and Naturalization: Trends and Laws, 1565–1882." JF-106.

_____. "Immigration and Naturalization: Trends and Laws, 1882–1924." JF-159.

Curran, Joan Ferris. "Numbering Your Genealogy: Sound and Simple Systems." BM-126.

Dearborn, David C. "An Introduction to Italian Church Records." VT-13.

_____. "Tracing Your Italian Ancestry." FW-04.

Galli, Jonathan D. "La Famiglia: Investigating Your Italian Ancestry." NE-54.

_____. "Preparing for Your Trip to Italy." VT-44.

Joslyn, Roger D. "19th Century Passenger Arrival Lists and Naturalization Records." HTX-185.

Lener, Dewayne J. "Italians in the Gulf Coast States and Arkansas." HTX-186.

_____. "Our Italian Heritage: Finding it in America and Italy." SL-73.

Mills, Elizabeth Shown. "Documentation! (How to Avoid Asking 'Where in the Sam Hill Did I Get that From?')." SW-72.

Polakoff, Eileen. "Welcome to the Golden Door—Immigrant Research in New York City." HTX-135.

Reisinger, Joy. "Catholic Church Records: What They Are and Aren't, Where to Find Them, and How to Use Them." HTX-102.

Remington, Gordon L. "Trouble Below Deck: Printed Passenger Lists." NTN-168.

Roberts, Jayare. "Ellis Island Research and the Nationwide Indexing Project." HTX-162.

_____. "The Italian-American Experience." HTX-44.

_____. "Using Passenger Arrival Records, 1820–1950." SW-101.

Rose, Keith F. "Italians in Virginia and Neighboring States: The Silent Settlers." RVA-59.

Schlyter, Daniel M. "European Passenger Lists." SL-107.

Smith, Marian L. "Immigration and Naturalization Service Records for Genealogists." RVA-33.

Sturdevant, Katherine Scott. "The Immigrant Experience: From Arrival to Assimilation." SD-80.

Szucs, Loretto Dennis. "Naturalization Records." NE-52.

Warren, James W. "Still Unpublished After All These Years? Writing Your Family History in Small, Manageable Pieces." NTN-116.

Case Studies
Carmack, Sharon DeBartolo. "The Genealogical Use of Social History: An Italian-American Example." *National Genealogical Society Quarterly* 79 (December 1991): 283–88.

_____. "Immigrant Women and Family Planning: Historical Clues for Genealogical Research." *National Genealogical Society Quarterly* 84 (June 1996): 102–114.

_____. "Panunzio's Deportation Cases of 1919–20: A Neglected Source and an Index." *National Genealogical Society Quarterly* 83 (December 1995): 293–300.

_____. "Using Social Security Records to Test an Italian-American Family Tradition." *National Genealogical Society Quarterly* 77 (December 1989): 256–59.

Dearborn, David Curtis. "Looking-Glass Del Vecchios of Moltrasio and New York: A Case Study in Tracing Italian Ancestors." *NEHGS NEXUS* 8 (1991): 198–200.

Fields, Joan and Donald Fields. "Avellino in Boston: An Italian-American Sampler." *NEHGS NEXUS* 8 (1991):194–197.

_____. "Avellino in Boston: An Italian-American Sampler, Part Two. Mining Reppucci Gold in the Hills of Avellino." *NEHGS NEXUS* 13 (1996): 66–69.

Social Histories, Customs, Folkways
Antinoro-Polizzi, Joseph and Angeline Guzzetta-Jones, eds. *Grandmother Said it Best: A Treasury of Italian Proverbs*. Tallevast, FL: Ausonia Press, 1980.

Balch Institute for Ethnic Studies. *Italian-American Traditions: Family and Community*. Philadelphia, 1985.

Barzini, Luigi. *The Italians: A Full-Length Portrait Featuring Their Manners and Morals*. New York: Atheneum, 1964.

Bell, Rudolph M. *Fate and Honor, Family and Village: Demographic and Cultural Change in Rural Italy Since 1800*. Chicago: University of Chicago Press, 1979.

Biagi, Ernest. *Italian Name-Places in the United States*. Philadelphia: 1970.

Bianco, Carla. *The Two Rosettos*. Bloomington, IN: Indiana University Press, 1974.

Bonville, William J. *Sicilian Walks: Exploring the History and Culture of the Two Sicilies*. Bedford, MA: Mills and Sanderson, 1988.

Calvino, Italo. *Italian Folktales*. New York: Pantheon Books, 1980.

Campisi, Paul J. "Ethnic Family Patterns: The Italians in the United States." *American Journal of Sociology* 53 (1948): 443–49.

Caroli, Betty Boyd. *Immigrants Who Returned Home*. New York: Chelsea House Publishers, 1990.

_____, et al., eds. *The Italian Immigrant Woman in North America*. Toronto: The Multicultural History Society of Ontario, 1978.

Catanzaro, Raimondo. *Men and Respect: A Social History of the Sicilian Mafia*. New York: The Free Press, 1988.

Child, Irving L. *Italian or American: The Second Generation in Conflict*. New Haven: Yale University Press, 1943.

Cinel, Dino. *From Italy to San Francisco: The Immigrant Experience*. Stanford, CA: Stanford University Press, 1982.

Cohen, Miriam. *Workshop to Office: Two Generations of Italian Women in New York City, 1900–1950*. Ithaca, NY: Cornell University Press, 1992.

Cordasco, Francesco. *Studies in Italian American Social History*. New York: Rowman and Littlefield, 1975.

Cornelisen, Ann. *Women of the Shadows: A Study of the Wives and Mothers of Southern Italy*. New York: Penguin Books, 1991.

Costantino, Mario and Lawrence Gambella. *The Italian Way: Aspects of Behavior, Attitudes, and Customs of the Italians*. Lincolnwood, IL: Passport Books, 1996.

Covello, Leonard. *The Social Background of the Italo-American School Child*. Leiden, Netherlands: E.J. Brill, 1967.

Daniels, Roger. *Coming to America: A History of Immigration and Ethnicity in American Life*. New York: HarperCollins, 1990.

DeConde, Alexander. *Half Bitter, Half Sweet: An Excursion into Italian-American History*. New York: Charles Schribner's Sons, 1971.

DeMarco, William M. *Ethnics and Enclaves: Boston's Italian North End*. Ann Arbor, MI: UMI Research Press, 1981.

di Leonardo, Micaela. *The Varieties of Ethnic Experience: Kinship, Class, and Gender Among California Italian Americans*. Ithaca: Cornell University Press, 1984.

Dillon, Richard. *North Beach: The Italian Heart of San Francisco*. Novato, CA: Presidio Press, 1985.

"Do Our Genes Determine Which Foods We Should Eat?" *Newsweek*, 9 August 1993.

Douglass, William A. *Emigration in a South Italian Town*. New Brunswick: Rutgers University Press, 1984.

Ets, Marie Hall. *Rosa: The Life of an Italian Immigrant*. Minneapolis: University of Minnesota, 1970.

Eula, Michael J. *Between Peasant and Urban Villager: Italian-Americans of New Jersey and New York, 1880–1980*. New York: Peter Lang, 1993.

Foerster, Robert. *The Italian Emigration of Our Times*. Cambridge: Harvard University Press, 1919.

Fox, Stephen. *The Unknown Internment: An Oral History of the Relocation of Italian Americans During World War II*. Boston: Twayne Publishers, 1990.

Fucilla, Joseph G. *Our Italian Surnames*. Baltimore: Genealogical Publishing Co., 1987.

Gabaccia, Donna. *From the Other Side: Women, Gender, and Immigrant Life in the United States, 1820–1990*. Bloomington, IN: Indiana University Press, 1994.

Gallo, Patrick J. *Old Bread, New Wine: A Portrait of the Italian-Americans*. Chicago: Nelson-Hall, 1981.

Gambino, Richard. *Blood of My Blood: The Dilemma of the Italian-Americans.* New York: Doubleday, 1974.

Handlin, Oscar. *The Uprooted.* 2d ed. Boston: Little, Brown, and Co., 1973.

Harrison, Barbara Grizzuti. *Italian Days.* New York: Ticknor and Fields, 1989.

Hearder, H. and D. P. Waley. *A Short History of Italy.* New York: Cambridge University Press, 1963.

Iorizzo, Luciano J. and Salvatore Mondello. *The Italian-Americans.* Rev. ed. New York: Twayne Publishers, 1980.

Johnson, Kevin Orlin. *Why Do Catholics Do That?: A Guide to the Teachings and Practices of the Catholic Church.* New York: Ballantine Books, 1994.

Kertzer, David I. *Family Life in Central Italy, 1880–1910: Sharecropping, Wage Labor, and Coresidence.* New Brunswick, NJ: Rutgers University Press, 1984.

_____ and Richard P. Saller, eds. *The Family in Italy from Antiquity to the Present.* New Haven: Yale University Press, 1991.

Kessner, Thomas. *The Golden Door: Italian and Jewish Immigrant Mobility in New York City, 1880–1915.* New York: Oxford University Press, 1977.

LaGumina, Salvatore J. *From Steerage to Suburb: Long Island Italians.* New York: Center for Migration Studies, 1988.

Levi, Carlo. *Christ Stopped at Eboli.* Reprint. Alexandria, VA: Time Life Books, 1982.

Lopez, Jadwiga, ed. *Christmas in Italy.* Chicago: World Book-Childcraft, 1979.

Lopreato, Joseph. *Italian Americans.* Austin: University of Texas, 1970.

Magnaghi, Russell M. "Louisiana's Italian Immigrants Prior to 1870." *Louisiana History* 27 (Winter 1986): 43–68.

Malpezzi, Frances M. and William M. Clements. *Italian–American Folklore.* Little Rock, AR: August House, 1992.

Mangione, Jerre. *Mount Allegro.* New York: Hill and Wang, 1952.

_____ and Ben Morreale. *La Storia: Five Centuries of the Italian American Experience.* New York: HarperCollins, 1992.

McCormick, C.A. and J. Colacicchi. *Life in an Italian Town.* Lincolnwood, IL: National Textbook Co., 1989.

Moquin, Wayne, et al., eds. *A Documentary History of the Italian Americans.* New York: Praeger Publishers, 1975.

Nelli, Humbert S. *From Immigrants to Ethnics: The Italian Americans.* New York: Oxford University Press, 1983.

_____. *Italians in Chicago, 1880–1930.* New York: Oxford University Press, 1970.

Orsi, Robert Anthony. *The Madonna of 115th Street: Faith and Community in Italian Harlem, 1880–1950.* New Haven: Yale University Press, 1985.

Perilli, Giovanni. *Colorado and the Italians in Colorado.* Denver: Smith Brooks Press, 1922.

Quadagno, Jill S. "The Italian American Family." In *Ethnic Families in America: Patterns and Variations.* Charles Mindel and Robert Habenstein, eds. New York: Elsevier-North Holland, 1981.

Ragucci, Antoinette T. "Italian Americans." In *Ethnicity and Medical Care.* Alan Harwood, ed. Cambridge: Harvard University Press, 1981.

Rolle, Andrew. *The Immigrant Upraised: Italian Adventurers and Colonists in an Expanding America.* Norman, OK: University of Oklahoma Press, 1968.

_____. *The Italian Americans: Troubled Roots.* Norman, OK: University of Oklahoma Press, 1980.

Rotunno, Marie and Monica McGoldrick. "Italian Families." In *Ethnicity and Family Therapy.* Monica McGoldrick, et al., eds. New York: Guilford Press, 1982.

Sartorio, Enrico C. *Social and Religious Life of Italians in America.* Clifton, NJ: Augustus M. Kelley Publisher, 1974.

Schiavo, Giovanni. *The Italians in America Before the Civil War.* New York: Vigo Press, 1934.

Schoener, Allon. *The Italian Americans.* New York: Macmillan Publishing Co., 1987.

Sforza, Carlo. *The Real Italians: A Study in European Psychology.* New York: Columbia University Press, 1942.

Smith, Denis Mack. *Italy: A Modern History.* Ann Arbor: University of Michigan Press, 1969.

Taylor, David A. and John Alexander Williams, eds. *Old Ties, New Attachments: Italian-American Folklife in the West.* Washington, DC: Library of Congress, 1992.

Thernstrom, Stephen, ed. *Harvard Encyclopedia of American Ethnic Groups.* Cambridge: Belknap Press, 1980.

Tomasi, Lydio. *The Italian American Family.* New York: Center for Migration Studies, 1972.

Weaver, Glenn. *The Italian Presence in Colonial Virginia.* New York: Center for Migration Studies, 1988.

Williams, Phyllis H. *South Italian Folkways in Europe and America.* New Haven: Yale University Press, 1938.

Works Progress Administration. *The Italians of New York.* New York: Random House, 1938.

Yans-McLaughlin, Virginia. *Family and Community: Italian Immigrants in Buffalo, 1880–1930.* Ithaca, NY: Cornell University Press, 1977.

Zuccotti, Susan. *The Italians and the Holocaust.* New York: Basic Books, 1987.

Passenger Ships, Steerage, and the Immigrant Experience

Abbott, Edith. *Immigration: Select Documents and Case Records.* Chicago: University of Chicago Press, 1924.

Anuta, Michael J. *Ships of Our Ancestors.* Menominee: MI: Ships of Our Ancestors, Inc. 1983.

Brandenburg, Broughton. *Imported Americans.* New York: F.A. Stokes Co., 1904.

Kludas, Arnold. *Great Passenger Ships of the World.* 5 vols. Cambridge: Stephens, 1975–77.

Marshall, Edward. "Makes Six Ocean Trips to Study Steerage and Reform." *New York Times*, Sunday, 30 November 1913, Part VI, page 10.

Price, Willard. "What I Learned by Traveling from Naples to New York in the Steerage." *The Italians: Social Background of an American Group.* Edited by Eugene Bucchioni and Francesco Cordasco. Clifton, NJ: Augustus M. Kelley Publ., 1974. Originally published in *World Outlook* 3 (October 1917): 3–5, 14.

Smith, Eugene W. *Passenger Ships of the World Past and Present.* Boston: George H. Dean Co., 1978.

"Steerage Report Stirs Ocean Liners." *New York Times*, Wednesday, 15 December 1909, page 3, column 4.

Steiner, Edward A. *On the Trail of the Immigrant.* 5th ed. New York: Fleming H. Revell Co., 1906.

Ellis Island

Bass, Thomas A. "A New Life Begins for the Island of Hope and Tears." *Smithsonian* (June 1990).

Bolino, August C. *The Ellis Island Source Book.* Washington, DC: Kensington Historical Press, 1985.

Chermayeff, Ivan, Fred Wasserman, and Mary J. Shapiro. *Ellis Island: An Illustrated History of the Immigrant Experience*. New York: Macmillan Publishing Co., 1991.

Dunne, Thomas and Wilton Tifft. *Ellis Island*. New York: W.W. Norton and Co., Inc. 1971.

Freeman, Allen. "Ellis Island Revisited." *Historic Preservation* (Sept–Oct 1990).

Hall, Alice J. "New Life for Ellis Island." *National Geographic* (September 1990).

Holzer, Harold. "Ellis Island's Rebirth." *Americana* (Sept–Oct 1990).

Island of Hope—Island of Tears: The Story of Ellis Island and the American Immigration Experience. Video. New York: The Ellis Island Immigration Museum Film, 1990.

Kinney, Doris G. "Reopening the Gateway to America." *Life* (September 1990).

Oxford, Edward "Hope, Tears, and Remembrance" and "A Treasure Rescued." *American History Illustrated* (October 1990).

Pitkin, Thomas M. *Keepers of the Gate: A History of Ellis Island*. New York: New York University Press, 1975.

Shapiro, Mary J. *Gateway to Liberty: The Story of the Statue of Liberty and Ellis Island*. New York: Vintage Books, 1986.

Szucs, Loretto Dennis. *Ellis Island: Gateway to America*. Salt Lake City: Ancestry Publishing, 1986.

Tifft, Wilton S. *Ellis Island*. Chicago: Contemporary Books, Inc. 1990.

Cookbooks with Italian Local History and Customs

Barolini, Helen. *Festa: Recipes and Recollections of Italian Holidays*. New York: Harcourt Brace, 1988.

Barr, Nancy Verde. *We Called It Macaroni: An American Heritage of Southern Italian Cooking*. New York: Alfred A. Knopf, 1990.

Field, Carol. *Celebrating Italy*. New York: William Morrow and Co., 1990.

Harris, Valentina. *Regional Italian Cooking*. New York: Pantheon Books, 1986.

Roden, Claudia. *The Good Food of Italy Region by Region*. New York: Alfred A. Knopf, 1990.

Root, Waverly. *The Food of Italy*. New York: Vintage Books, 1971.

Atlases and Travel Guides with Italian History
Baedeker's Italy. Turin: G. Canale, 1991.

The Hatchette Guide to Italy. New York: Pantheon Books, 1988.

Rand McNally Road Atlas of Italy. Chicago: Rand McNally and Co., 1989.

Thompson, Ian. *Southern Italy*. New York: Independent Traveler, 1990.

Italian-American Narrative Family Histories
Baily, Samuel L. and Franco Ramella, eds. *One Family, Two Worlds: An Italian Family's Correspondence Across the Atlantic, 1901–1922*. New Brunswick, NJ: Rutgers University Press, 1988.

Carmack, Sharon DeBartolo. *The Ebetino and Vallarelli Family History: Italian Immigrants to Westchester County, New York*. Decorah, IA: Anundsen Publishing, 1990.

Roy, Elissandra N., ed. *The House of Flowers: La Casa di Fiore, 1890–1990*. Arlington, VA: Caesar Frank Fiore, 1990.

Talese, Gay. *Unto the Sons*. New York: Alfred Knopf Publishers, 1992.

Examples of Non-Italian Family History Narratives
Cashin, Joan. "'Since the War Broke Out': The Marriage of Kate and William McLure." In *Divided Houses: Gender and the Civil War*, ed. by Catherine Clinton and Nina Silber.

Frazier, Ian. *Family*. New York: Farrar, Straus and Giroux, 1994.

Harrell, Carolyn L. *Kith and Kin: A Portrait of a Southern Family, 1630–1934*. Macon, GA: Mercer University Press, 1984.

McFarland, Gerald. *A Scattered People: An American Family Moves West*. New York: Pantheon, 1985.

Nagel, Paul C. *The Lees of Virginia: Seven Generations of an American Family*. Oxford University Press, 1990.

Periodicals
Ambassador, National Italian American Foundation, 666 11th St., NW, Suite 800, Washington, DC 20001-4596.

Dall'Italia, P.O. Box 1340, New York, NY 10131-0574.

Fra Noi: Chicagoland's Italian American Voice, 480 N. Wolf Rd., Northlake, IL 60164-1667.

Italian-American Digest, The Italian Voice of the South, 1608 S. Salcedo St., New Orleans, LA 70125.

Italian Americana, University of Rhode Island, College of Continuing Education, 80 Washington St., Providence, RI 02903.

ITALY, *Italy*, 138 Wooster St., New York, NY 10012.

Il Poplo Italiano. 21 S. Chalfonte Ave., Box 447, Atlantic City, NJ 08401.

Journal of Italian Food and Wine and Travel, 609 West 114ᵗʰ St., New York, NY 10025.

POINTers: The American Journal of Italian Genealogy. Pursuing Our Italian Names Together, P.O. Box 2977, Palos Verdes, CA 90274.

Novels with Italian-American Social History and Customs
DiDonato, Pietro. *Christ in Concrete*. Indianapolis: Bobbs-Merrill, 1934.

Fiore, Carmen Anthony. *Vendetta Mountain*. Princeton, NJ: Townhouse Publishers, 1987.

Manes, Rose Tavino. *Prima Vera: Springtime*. Ft. Lauderdale, FL: Ashley Books, 1991.

Pagano, Jo. *Golden Wedding*. New York: Random House, 1943.

_____. *The Paesanos*. Boston: Little, Brown, and Co., 1940.

Puzo, Mario. *The Fortunate Pilgrim*. New York: Bantam Books, 1985.

_____. *The Godfather*. New York: Signet Books, 1969.

_____. *The Sicilian*. New York: Bantam Books, 1985.

Stewart, Fred Mustard. *Century*. New York: Signet Books, 1981.

_____. *Ellis Island*. New York: Signet Books, 1983.

Oral History Interviewing Guides
Akeret, Robert U. *Family Tales, Family Wisdom: How to Gather the Stories of a Lifetime and Share Them with Your Family*. New York: Henry Holt, 1991.

Davis, Cullom, Kathryn Back and Kay MacLean. *Oral History: From Tape to Type*. Chicago: American Library Association, 1977.

Fletcher, William. *Recording Your Family History: A Guide to Preserving Oral History Using Audio and Video Tape*. Berkeley: Ten Speed Press, 1989.

Writing and Publishing Guides
Alexander, Dana Jordan and Amy Shea. *Lasting Memories: A Guide to Writing Your Family History*. Charlotte, NC: Generations Publications, 1996.

Barnes, Donald R. and Richard S. Lackey. *Write it Right: A Manual for Writing Family Histories and Genealogies*. Ocala, FL: Lyon Press, 1983.

Cheney, Theodore A. Rees. *Writing Creative Nonfiction*. Cincinnati: Writer's Digest Books, 1987.

Curran, Joan Ferris. "Numbering Your Genealogy: Sound and Simple Systems." *National Genealogical Society Quarterly* 79 (September 1991): 183–93.

Franklin, Jon. *Writing for Story: Craft Secrets of Dramatic Nonfiction*. New York: Mentor Books, 1986.

Gerard, Philip. *Creative Nonfiction: Researching and Crafting Stories of Real Life*. Cincinnati: Story Press, 1996.

Gouldrup, Lawrence P. *Writing the Family Narrative*. Salt Lake City: Ancestry Publishing, 1987.

_____. *Writing the Family Narrative Workbook*. Salt Lake City: Ancestry Publishing, 1993.

Hatcher, Patricia Law. *Producing a Quality Family History*. Salt Lake City: Ancestry Publishing, 1996.

Hemley, Robin. *Turning Life into Fiction*. Cincinnati: Story Press, 1994.

Herman, Jeff. *Insider's Guide to Book Editors, Publishers, and Literary Agents*. Rocklin, CA: Prima Publishing, 1996.

Hughes, Ann Hege. "Preparing Manuscripts for Offset Printing." *Association of Professional Genealogists Quarterly* 8 (June 1993): 31.

_____. "Publishing Genealogical Research: Commercially and Privately." *Association of Professional Genealogists Quarterly* 5 (Fall 1990): 60.

Martin, Rhona. *Writing Historical Fiction*. New York: St. Martin's Press, 1988.

Noble, William. *Show, Don't Tell*. Middlebury, VT: Paul S. Eriksson Publisher, 1991.

Polking, Kirk. *Writing Family Histories and Memoirs*. Cincinnati: Betterway Books, 1995.

Poynter, Dan. *The Self-Publishing Manual: How to Write, Print, and Sell Your Own Book*. 8th ed. Santa Barbara, CA: Para Publishing, 1995.

Sturdevant, Katherine Scott. "Documentary Editing for Family Historians." *Association of Professional Genealogists Quarterly* 5 (Spring 1990): 3.

Talese, Gay and Barbara Loundsberry. *Writing Creative Nonfiction: The Literature of Reality*. New York: HarperCollins, 1996.

Writer's Market. Cincinnati: Writer's Digest Books, annual.

Basic How-To Genealogy Books

Crandall, Ralph. *Shaking Your Family Tree*. Dublin, NH: Yankee Publishing Co., 1986.

Doane, Gilbert H. and James B. Bell. *Searching for Your Ancestors: The How and Why of Genealogy*. 6th ed. Minneapolis: The University of Minnesota Press, 1992.

Greenwood, Val D. *The Researcher's Guide to American Genealogy*. 2d ed. Baltimore: Genealogical Publishing Co., 1990.

Stryker-Rodda, Harriet. *How to Climb Your Family Tree*. Baltimore: Genealogical Publishing Co., 1987.

Szucs, Loretto Dennis and Sandra Hargreaves Luebking, eds. *The Source: A Guidebook of American Genealogy*. Rev. ed. Salt Lake City: Ancestry Publishing, 1996.